THE VOYAGE ALONE
IN THE YAWL 'ROB ROY'

Other Sailing Classics

The Voyage Alone
in the Yawl 'Rob Roy'

JOHN MacGREGOR

Edited with an Introduction by
Arthur Ransome

Grafton Books
A Division of the Collins Publishing Group
8 Grafton Street, London W1X 3LA

First published 1867
This edition published by Grafton Books 1987

British Library Cataloguing in Publication Data

MacGregor, John, *1825–1892*
The voyage alone in the yawl 'Rob Roy'.
1. Voyages and travels   2. Canoes and
canoing—English Channel
I. Title
910'.0916336   G490

ISBN 0-246-13176-4

Printed in Great Britain by
Robert Hartnoll (1985) Ltd
Bodmin Cornwall

CONTENTS

CONTENTS

vi

CONTENTS

ILLUSTRATIONS

MAPS

JOHN ("ROB ROY") MacGREGOR

JOHN MACGREGOR was one of those men who, like some actors, seem to have a magnetic attraction for limelight and live their whole lives in a glare of publicity. He became a public character as it were while still a baby. His father was Duncan MacGregor, born in 1787, ensign in the 72nd at thirteen, who fought in the Napoleonic wars, was wounded in Calabria in 1806, was fighting in Egypt in 1807, took part in the Walcheren expedition in 1809, married a daughter of Sir William Dick of Prestonfield near Edinburgh and in 1824, being under orders for India, as a Major in the 31st, went with his wife to Gravesend, where he took lodgings from which they could see the *Kent*, in which the regiment was to sail, lying at anchor in the river. Their first child, John MacGregor, was born on January 24, 1825, in these lodgings, close to the water, from which all his life he found it hard to keep away. On February 18, Mrs. MacGregor and her baby were carried aboard, and the *Kent* sailed next day. On March 1, when she was driving under storm staysail in the Bay of Biscay during a heavy westerly gale, she was found to be on fire. All efforts to put out the fire failed, and the loss of life would have been heavier even than it was if the burning *Kent* had not been sighted by a small brig, the *Cambria*, that stood by her and took aboard all who were able to escape. Of the 641 persons aboard, sixty-eight men of the regiment were lost, one woman and twenty-one children, besides sailors and some who were rescued but died after reaching the brig. The survivors, so closely packed below decks that it was said that a lighted candle instantly went out in the foul air, were brought through dreadful weather to Falmouth, where they arrived four days later. The MacGregors went to Scotland to recover from these trials, but presently sailed for London in a coasting steamship which lost her anchors and was drifting on the Newcome Sands off Lowestoft when the wind happily changed, thus giving the infant John MacGregor his second narrow escape. Foreshadowing the publicity that attended all he did, Miss Hannah More, the poet, then aged over eighty, sent him a pair of woolly socks of her own knitting and addressed a poem to him, beginning,

> Sweet babe, *twice* rescued from the yawning grave,
> The flames tremendous and the furious wave . . .

In August 1826, Duncan MacGregor, now Lieutenant-Colonel of the 93rd, the Sutherland Highlanders, sailed for the West Indies with his regiment, but this time did not take his wife with him. He returned in 1828, and thereafter the family moved with the regiment, and the schooling of John MacGregor and his brothers varied accordingly. Rob Roy (John MacGregor was so called as a child and took the name as a trademark for all his activities as a man) began playing with boats on a Northamptonshire canal, and, wherever he was, took every chance he had of going afloat. At the age of twelve, at Belfast, when the lifeboat was called for to go to a ship in distress, he ran to help in the launching, jumped in at the last moment, and went off to the rescue. At fifteen he had his third narrow escape from drowning, when a little iron cutter sank under him outside Kingstown harbour.

INTRODUCTION

He was never at a boarding school, but went as a day-boy to eight different schools, including the King's School at Canterbury when his father was stationed there. In 1838 his father was appointed Inspector General of the Irish Constabulary and went to live at Drumcondra, just outside Dublin. John MacGregor went to Dublin College and later, after some coaching at Liverpool, entered Trinity College, Cambridge, where he rowed in his College Eight, threw himself into Sunday-school work, boxing, and Bible-reading, and began writing for *Punch*, to which he contributed for many years, handing over the payments he received to the Ragged School Union. He was 24th Wrangler in 1847, when he left Cambridge and came to London to read for the Bar.

He was in Paris during the revolution of 1848. On July 7 of that year, staying with his father in Ireland, he wrote in his diary: "Carlyle, author of Cromwell's Life, etc., came to dinner last night. A young Scotchman, clever and *outré*, designedly careless, uses much strong language, but his epithets often twice over. Fond of fun and unaffected. Not happy looking." "Rob Roy" MacGregor was then twenty-three, and the "young Scotchman" was thirty years older. A few years before his death the diarist mentioned this meeting with Carlyle at Drumcondra as one of the important events of his life.

He early began to spend much time in foreign travel. In 1849 he made his first long journey in the Middle East, visiting Greece, Turkey, Syria, Palestine, and Egypt in the course of eight months. Characteristic entries in his diary are: "Aug. 8. Started in the grey dawn in our sailing boat to Gozo, fifteen miles. Stopped during the middle of the day at St. Paul's Bay, landing on the island of Selmone on which his ship was wrecked." "Aug. 10. Bathed and swam to the mainland the same course which St. Paul and his company must have escaped by. Read the account of the wreck in the Acts." Made daring by little knowledge, he even prepared and published a little book on Eastern music, picking up the tunes by ear, playing them on the flute, getting them sung and re-sung by a native orchestra and finally written down.

In 1850 he took his degree as M.A. at Cambridge, and in that year he with three other friends, all interested in the Ragged Schools, were discussing what could be done to find work for ragged boys when in the following year London would be full of visitors to the Great Exhibition. The four young men were walking arm-in-arm up the middle of Holborn Hill when one of them suggested shoe-blacking. MacGregor promptly formed a committee, persuaded Lord Ashley to be President, secured the good will of the police, and so launched the Shoeblack Society, which would have made him famous even if he had never thought of his canoes. There are not so many shoeblacks now as there were when I first came to London fifty years ago, but a few of the old red coats are still to be seen, and the whole organisation has been taken over by a firm of blacking manufacturers, though here and there you may even to-day find an elderly shoeblack who has at least heard the name of John MacGregor. He was ready to develop the idea still further, with the Messenger Boys (the Ragged School Shoeblack Society accepting responsibility for "any booked parcel to the amount of £3"). He suggested a corps of little girls to whiten doorsteps at a penny a step, and planned brigades of newspaper boys, knife sharpeners and window cleaners.

His interests multiplied. In May, 1853, he wrote: "Among the objects now claiming my best attention are The Protestant Alliance, the Protestant Defence Society, The Ragged School Union, the Shoeblacks, The Ragged School Shop, *The Band of Hope Review, The True Briton,* The Town Mission, The Open Air Mission, the Slavery Question, The Preventive and Reformatory School Society, The Lawyer's Prayer Union and the Mansfield Society." . . . Already, in 1852, a letter addressed to "Mr. MacGregor, Philanthropist, London," had reached him without delay.

He climbed Mont Blanc, Vesuvius, and Etna one after another, and duly wrote to *The Times* to let the world know what he had done. He lectured to a section of the British Association on early methods of propelling ships. Of a tour in Spain, undertaken to settle a question as to the invention of the steamship, he wrote that "it would clear away the cobwebs for a right good hard working winter, please God." He toured Norway with some friends and was much disappointed that it was not he but another member of the party who had the good fortune to be attacked by a pack of wolves. He always illustrated his diaries with his own sketches, and was presently illustrating Livingstone's "Travels and Researches in South Africa" (where he had never been). Livingstone wrote him an illuminating letter on his objects in pushing "our enterprise and our Christianity . . ." making the Zambesi "a path of lawful commerce by stimulating the tribes inhabiting its banks to engage in collecting and cultivating the raw materials of English manufacture." In 1858 he visited America and Canada, seeing much of negro preachers and noting that "There will be a Civil War about these slaves." In 1859 he visited Russia, made some lively sketches and, dramatising himself as always, was delighted to record that his was "the only Glengarry cap that had ever been seen at Nijni Novgorod." In Sweden he went down an iron mine and made use of the experience afterwards in a lecture that he characteristically entitled "Rob Roy Underground." Besides all this he was working at his profession as a lawyer, and published a book on "The Language of Specifications," an "Abridgment of the Specifications relating to Marine Propulsion," and "A Digest of the Patent Laws."

On his return from the Russian journey he became a Volunteer, joining the London Scottish, of which he became a bugler, and a fortnight later wrote in his diary, "Certainly my popularity in the corps is very dangerous to my modesty." A month after that he became Captain of the East Company. Two days later, not content with the name, he "got it changed to 'Central Company' by Lord Elcho and Committee." He then obtained for his company the right to wear the kilt, was presented by them with a sword and won the regimental prize for marksmanship. . . . Presently there is a note in his diary: "To Paris. In the kilt to Vincennes to visit the Tir Nationale for the National Rifle Association." It was while he was a Volunteer that he summed up his own character with disarming clearness of sight. He wrote, "The most careful, thoughtful and deliberate conviction about this is that quiet, unobtrusive, gentle, humble piety . . . never once speaking of oneself . . . is the way to be admired. I am perfectly well aware of this, and I know if I wished most of all to be thus prominent I should rightly guard myself against what I am very, very remarkable for; boastfulness, rude pride with vain self-praise, and a yielding to the quick impulse of exercising authority, telling of every success and omitting no chance of promoting myself before my friends, not to say before the public. The rapid and frequent pleasure of doing this is more enjoyed than the deep, calm sensation of being great, which a humble self-negation in these things would entail."

His natural genius for publicity, his instinctive show-manship was always of service to whatever cause he might happen to be advocating, and his enthusiasm for Volunteers, rifle-shooting, the kilt, and Glengarry caps was presently to be replaced by enthusiasm for something very different. Whatever he did, he always wanted to persuade everybody else to play "Follow my Leader!" and in 1865 he found a new interest that was to give the name Rob Roy a new meaning. He used to say that as long ago as 1848 the sight of an india-rubber boat had first set him thinking about canoes. In May 1865 he thought of a canoe voyage. He designed a canoe himself, remembering the North American and Kamchatkan canoes with double-ended paddles he had seen. On June 21 he went to see his canoe in the shed where she was being built (she had already been named, of course, the *Rob Roy*) and on June 27 she was ready. On July 9 he made a first ecstatic voyage on the Thames and at once, as in so many other affairs, turned urgent propagandist. On July 21 he attended the Wimbledon review of the Volunteers and "returned fully persuaded that the Canoe Club, of which prospectus is out today, is far better for fun, exercise and real amusement." In that year he made his first series of voyages in the canoe, put together his first canoe book, *A Thousand Miles in the Rob Roy Canoe on Twenty Lakes and Rivers of Europe*, with woodcuts from the author's drawings and a note on the title page that all profits were to go to the Shipwrecked Mariners Society and the National Lifeboat Institution, published it in January 1866, found a new edition needed at once, was given "a splendid 2¼ columns of unmixed praise in *The Times*" on April 15, noted on April 20, "2000 of my second edition sold in five days," and on May 17, "Third edition of my book came out to-day." Already in March he had lectured on the *Rob Roy* before the Institute of Naval Architects . . . "showed sails, paddle, etc., and put on dress." But this was not enough. The Canoe Club was founded with a dinner at the Star and Garter at Richmond, and just as unerring instinct had led him to ask Lord Ashley to be the first President of his Shoeblack Society in 1850, so now, sixteen years later, he persuaded the Prince of Wales to be the President of what was very soon to become The Royal Canoe Club, and is a flourishing institution to this day. I do not suppose any man ever sent so many of his countrymen to find their pleasure on the water. Branch after branch of the Canoe Club came into existence, welcomed by Rob Roy in person, ready to demonstrate the costume he had devised as most fitting for a canoeist, his paddle, and his latest canoe. The idea was simple. You took your canoe by steamboat to the Continent, by train or diligence or farm cart to the upper waters of your chosen river, and then descended, with current, tide, and tiny sail to help you, finding lodging for the night ashore. What more delightful form of foreign travel could undergraduates devise? And for those who could not afford to go so far, there were all the rivers of England to explore, while MacGregor himself, ahead of his proselytes, but not too far ahead, was for ever setting them new standards of romantic voyaging abroad. MacGregor inspired the *Inland Voyage* of Robert Louis Stevenson and Sir Walter Simpson in the *Cigarette* and the *Arethusa*. MacGregor inspired E. F. Knight (whose *The Falcon on the Baltic* and *The Cruise of the Alerte* are volumes 15 and 21 in The Mariners Library) and his friend C. S. Jerram to take Rob Roy canoes with them to France. More detailed accounts of MacGregor's canoe voyages must be left to a forthcoming volume of the Mariners Library which will be concerned with nothing else. The *Thousand Miles* book was followed in 1866 by *The Rob Roy on the Baltic* and in 1869 by *The Rob Roy on the Jordan, Nile, Red Sea and Gennesareth, etc.*

The Voyage Alone in the Yawl Rob Roy (1867) was a by-product of his canoeing propaganda. The Emperor Napoleon III had read of MacGregor's canoes, and wishing "to encourage a taste for the exploration of solitary streams and lonely currents among the youth of France" approved of a "Boat Exhibition" to be held in Paris with a regatta on the Seine. MacGregor immediately decided to sail in a boat of his own from London to the Exhibition, with a cargo of Protestant tracts, so that, with additional prestige, he could at the same time organise canoeing events in the regatta, bring the true faith to benighted Roman Catholics and collect material for further lectures and for another book, the profits from which should go to the training ships for boys, and thus further philanthropic ends and justify the spending of a delightful summer.

The voyage was thus conceived and carried out as a piece of showmanship. It was planned as a notable exploit, and a notable exploit it was indeed to take, in

Distributing tracts

1867, a 21-foot sailing-boat from Limehouse to Dover, thence to Boulogne and along the north coast of France to the Seine, up the Seine to Paris, down again to Havre, and from Havre across the Channel to Little-hampton, the Solent, and thence back to the Thames. In his journal he wrote the following summary. "1867. June 7. Started from Forrest's in my yawl *Rob Roy*, and on September 21 proudly brought her back after

three months and a half. Record of this in my book
'The Voyage Alone.' From then to Nov. 2 occupied in
writing the book. Dec. 14 my book came out. 1868.
Mar. 3. First lecture on The Voyage Alone." In the
letter he wrote on his arrival in Littlehampton after
crossing from Havre, a letter that is here printed as an
appendix to his book, he wrote, "A load is off my
mind—I had set myself a great feat to do, a greater one
now seen in the past than in prospect and I have been
allowed full gratification of success. Pride and satisfaction too much for such a worldly matter may supervene, but I must only guard against excess—there is a
legitimate amount allowable." And, at the end of the
letter, "I feel I have performed a feat and no more need
be added to it.—It is worthy of the Captain of the
Canoe Club and I am content."

He was, of course, careful to see that the feat did
not pass unnoticed. Instantly on arrival he wrote
to *The Times*, announcing what he had done, just as,
earlier, he had at once reported that he had climbed
the three mountains. He would have felt that any
"feat" was wasted that was not used in earning money,
not for himself but for the various causes he had made
his own. He set himself the task of earning £10,000
by lecturing on his voyages in canoes and in the little
yawl. In a single year he earned £4,160, and in due
course was able to record in his journal that he had
earned £10,042. Characteristically he notes that at the
end of the lecture which brought his earnings over the
£10,000 at which he had aimed, a boy and a girl
came on the platform wearing, like the stewards,
scarves of MacGregor tartan and presented him with
"a splendid bouquet of camellias." His natural show-

manship was carried into every detail of his lecturing. He would have a canoe, or a model of his boat, on the platform. A quick-change artist, he would slip behind a screen and emerge in the "uniform" he had devised for canoeing. Just as their scarlet coats had helped in the success of his shoeblacks, so now the canoeist appeared in a scarlet Norfolk jacket. Lecturing on his canoe voyages on the Nile and the Jordan, he appeared on the platform in something like Arab costume, with a long Turkish pipe, and after telling the story of the crocodile into whose gaping mouth he had looked, contrived the appearance of a crocodile on a screen behind the lecturer, with himself on its back and mottoes, "God Save the Queen!" and "Long life to . . ." whatever the charity, society or institute for the benefit of which he was speaking. Such was his popularity that years later whole audiences at meetings at which he was not present would rise to their feet and cheer at the mention of his name. His son-in-law, Dr. MacGregor-Morris, has told me how, invited to a dinner, Rob Roy MacGregor went to the wrong house, where his astonished hosts were so delighted to have him at their table that they kept secret his mistake so that he did not learn what he had done till he came home late at night after enthralling them for hours.

MacGregor's instinctive and indefatigable showmanship, valuable as it was in making sure that people heard whatever he had to say, would not have given him his important place in the history of cruising in small boats if he had not had the fortunate gift of making his pleasures infectious. "I am in extreme enjoyment," he kept saying in one way and another. It was obviously true, and man after man listened and determined to put to sea. "All Hail 'The Voyage Alone'!" wrote the eccentric Middleton, bought him *The Kate*, a little yawl like the *Rob Roy*, persuaded MacGregor to inspect the boat and to give him good advice, and set off to circumnavigate England. The Rev. William Forwell, a Presbyterian Minister of Broughty Ferry, after "reading Mr. MacGregor's delightful description of his *Voyage Alone in the Yawl Rob Roy*," had built for him a little lugger, 20 feet over all, 19 feet on the keel and, with his 14 year old son, cruised in fourteen weeks from Broughty Ferry to Calais and back. Directly and indirectly MacGregor has been inspiring such voyages ever since.

MacGregor made one more voyage in the yawl in the summer of 1868, up the Thames and then by canal and the rivers Wey and Arun to Littlehampton and so to Portsmouth, but he still thought canoeing "the best of all modes of travelling for true enjoyment, exercise and sight-seeing at the same time" and was busy making ready for the most famous of his canoe voyages, described in *Rob Roy on the Jordan*. In 1871 he sold the yawl *Rob Roy* to a man in Australia, and was presently writing in his journal that he had "heard grand accounts of arrival of dear old yawl at Melbourne." In September he took a canoe to Holland made interesting notes but did not think it worth while to make a book out of them. In 1872 he visited the Shetlands. In 1873 he left his canoe at home and voyaged to the Azores in a steamship. Walking the deck on August 25, he made up his mind to propose marriage to a lady whom "he had loved eight years in silence." He came straight home from Graciosa, where the vessel called, proposed on arrival and was married on December 4 with a guard of honour of boys from the *Chichester* training ship and a detachment of red-coated shoeblacks, a thousand people in the church and crowds in the street outside. After his marriage he attempted no more "feats" (though he never lost interest in the Royal Canoe Club and small boats) but went on lecturing all over the country for the benefit of institutions he thought deserving. He organised memorials to Lord Shaftesbury, Gordon, Tyndale, and the Smithfield martyrs. He had settled in a house at Blackheath, and was living there with his wife and daughters when, in 1888, it became clear that he who had hardly known any but the robustest health was seriously ill. He set out on a sea voyage to the North Cape but grew rapidly weaker and had to return from Trondhjeim. He moved to Boscombe, near Bournemouth, where he was attended by Dr. T. B. Scott, the doctor to whom another canoeist and sailor, Robert Louis Stevenson of the *Arethusa*, had dedicated *Underwoods* two years before. He died on July 15, 1892, aged sixty-seven.

The text that follows is that of the second edition, from which a good deal of matter irrelevant to the voyage and of little interest to-day has been removed. In an appendix is printed the illustrated letter written by John MacGregor at Littlehampton, on his arrival there from Havre in July 1867. He had asked in the letter that it should be preserved so that he could make use of it, but internal evidence suggests that it was temporarily lost and that he had to write the chapters giving his account of the crossing without being able to consult it. In certain details it differs from the book. By the time MacGregor came to write his book he had taken the little yawl to Cowes, had made a triumphal appearance there, and, no doubt, had had to tell the story of the crossing many times. Stories many times retold have a way of editing themselves, not always for the better. I have to thank Dr. MacGregor-Morris for letting me see MacGregor's note-books and other most interesting relics and for this letter of his father-in-law's, which, written within a few hours of his stepping ashore, preserves unblunted the exultant happiness of its author.

ARTHUR RANSOME

PREFACE

In the earlier part of this voyage, and where it was most wished for, along the dangerous coast of France, fine weather came.

Next there was an amphibious interlude in the journey to Paris, while the *Rob Roy* sailed inland.

Thence her course over the sea brought the yawl across the broad Channel to Cowes and its Regattas, and to rough water in dark nights of thunder, until once more in the Thames and up the Medway she was under bright skies again.

Cooking and sleeping on board, the writer performed the whole journey without any companion; and perhaps this log of the voyage will show that it was not only delightful to the lone sailor, but useful to others.

CHAPTER I

Project — On the stocks — Profile — Afloat alone — Smart lads —
Swinging — Anchors — Happy boys — Sea reach — Good looks —
Peep below—Important trifles—In the well—Chart—Watch on
deck—Eating an egg—Storm sail.

It was a strange and pleasant life for me all the summer,
sailing entirely alone by sea and river fifteen hundred
miles, and with its toils, perils, and adventures heartily
enjoyed.

The two preceding summers I had paddled alone in
an oak canoe, first through central Europe, and next
over Norway and Sweden; but though both of these
voyages were delightful, they had still the drawback,
that progress was mainly dependent on muscular effort,
that food must be had from shore, and that I could not
sleep on the water.

In devising plans to make the pleasure of a voyage
complete then, many cogitations were had last winter,
and these resulted in a beautiful little sailing-boat; and
once afloat in this, the water was my road, my home,
my very world, for a long and splendid summer.

The perfect success of these three voyages has been
due mainly to the careful preparation for them in the
minute details which are too often neglected. To take
pains about these is a pleasure to a man with a boating
mind, but it is also a positive necessity if he would ensure success; nor can we wonder at the fate of some who
get swamped, smashed, stove in, or turned over, when
we see them go adrift in a craft which had been huddled
into being by some builder ignorant of what is wanted

for the sailor traveller, and is launched on unknown waters without due preparation for what may come.

I resolved to have a thoroughly good sailing-boat—the largest that could be well managed in rough weather by one strong man, and with every bolt, cleat, sheave, and rope well-considered in relation to the questions: How will this work in a squall?—on a rock?—in the dark?—or in a rushing tide?—a crowded lock; not to say in a storm?

The internal arrangements of my boat having been fully settled with the advantage of the canoe experiences, the yacht itself was designed by Mr. John White, of Cowes—and who could do it better? She was to be first *safe*, next *comfortable*, and then *fast*. If, indeed, you have two men aboard, one to pick up the other when he falls over, then you may put the last of the above three qualities first, but not prudently when there is only one man to do the whole.

The *Rob Roy* was built by Messrs. Forrest, of Limehouse, the builders for the Royal National Lifeboat Institution, and so she is a lifeboat to begin with. Knowing how much I might have to depend on oars now and then, my inclination was to limit her length to about eighteen feet, but Mr. White said that twenty-one feet would "take care of herself in a squall." Therefore that length was agreed upon, and the decision was never regretted; still I should by no means advise any increase of these dimensions.

One great advantage of the larger size was that it enabled me to carry in the cabin of my yawl, another boat, a little dingey* or punt, to go ashore by, to take

* Shown by dotted lines in the sketch at p. 33. The *Rob Roy* is of about four tons' burthen, but "tons," we know well, mean one does not know what.

exercise in, and to use for refuge in last resource if shipwrecked, for this dingey also I determined should be a
lifeboat, and yet only eight feet long. The childhood of
this little boat was somewhat unhappy, and as she grew
into shape she was quizzed unmercifully, and people
shook their heads very wisely, as they did at the first
Rob Roy canoe. Now that we can reckon about two
hundred of such canoes, and now that this little dingey
has proved a complete success and an unspeakable convenience, the laugh may be forgotten. However, ridicule of new things often does good if it begets caution in
changes, and stimulates improvement. Good things get
even benefit from ridicule, which may shake off the
plaster and paint, though it will not shiver the stone.

Thoroughly to enjoy a cruise with only two such
dumb companions as have been described, it is of importance that the man who is to be with them should
also be adapted for his place. He must have good
health and good spirits, and a passion for the sea. He
must learn to rise, eat, drink, and sleep, as the water or
winds decree, and not his watch. He must have wits to
regard at once the tide, breeze, waves, chart, buoys, and
lights; also the sails, Pilot-book, and compass; and more
than all, to scan the passing vessels, and to cook, and
eat, and drink in the midst of all. With such pressing
and varied occupations, he has no time to feel "lonely,"
and indeed, he passes fewer hours in the week alone than
many a busy man in chambers. Of all those I have met
with who have travelled on land or sea alone, not one
has told me it was "lonely," though some who have
never tried the plan as a change upon life in a crowd,
may fear its unknown pleasures. As for myself, on this
voyage I could scarcely "get a moment to myself," and

there was always an accumulation of things to be done, or read, or thought over, when a vacant half-hour could be had. The man who will feel true loneliness, is he who has one sailor with him, or a "pleasant companion" soon pumped dry, for he has isolation without freedom all day (and night too), and a tight cramp on the mind. With a dozen kindred spirits in a yacht, indeed, it is another matter; then you have freedom and company, and (if you are not the owner) you are not slaves of the skipper, but still you are *sailed* and *carried*, as passive travellers, and perhaps after all you had better be in a big steamer at once—the Cunard's or the P. and O., with a hundred passengers—real life and endless variety. However, each man to his taste; it is not easy to judge for others, but let us hope, that after listening to this log of a voyage alone you will not call it "lonely."

The *Rob Roy* is a yawl-rig, so as to place the sailor between the sails for "handiness." She is double-skinned to make her staunch and dry below, and she is full-decked to keep out the sea above. She has an iron keel and kelson to resist a bump on rocks, and with four water-tight compartments to limit its effects if once stove in. Her cabin is comfortable to sleep in, but only as arranged when anchored for the purpose:—sleep at sea is forbidden to her crew. Her internal arrangements for cooking, reading, writing, provisions, stores, and cargo, are quite different from those of any other yacht; all of them are specially devised, and all well done; and now on the 7th of June, at 3 p.m., she is hastily launched, her ton and a half of pig-iron is put on board for ballast, the luggage and luxuries for a three months' voyage are loaded in, her masts are stepped, the sails are bent, the flags unfold to the breeze, the line to shore

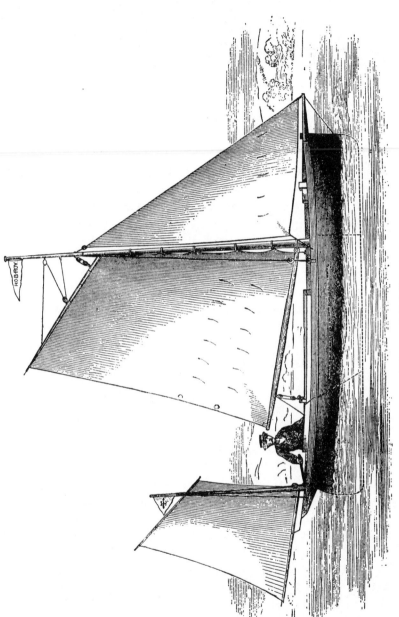

C

The yawl *Rob Roy*

is slipped, and we are sailing from Woolwich, never to have any person aboard in her progress but the captain, until she returns to the builders' yard.

Often as a boy I had thought of the pleasure of being one's own master in one's own boat; but the reality far exceeded the imagination of it, and it was not a transient pleasure. Next day it was stronger, and so to the end, until at last, only duty forced me reluctantly from my floating freehold to another home founded on London clay, sternly immovable, and with the quarter's rent to pay.

At Erith next day the Canoe Club held its first sailing match, when five little paddling craft set up their bamboo masts and pure white sails, and scudded along in a rattling breeze, and twice crossed the Thames. They were so closely matched that the winner was only by a few seconds first. Then a Club dinner toasted the prizemen, and "farewell," "bon voyage" to the captain, who retired on board for the first sleep in his yawl.

The Sunday service on board the Training-ship *Worcester*, at Erith, is a sight to see and to remember. The bell rings and boats arrive, some of them with ladies. Here in the 'tween decks, with airy ports open, and glancing water seen through them, are 100 fresh-cheeked manly boys, the future captains of *Taepings* and *Ariels*, and as fine specimens of the gentleman sailor-lad as any Englishman would wish to see. Such neatness and order without nonsense or prim awe. Health and brightness of boyhood, with seamen's smartness and silence: I hope they do not get too much trigono-metry. However, for the past week they have been skurrying up aloft "to learn the ropes," skylarking

34

among the rigging for play, and rowing and cricketing to expand muscle and limb; and now on the day of rest they sing beautifully to the well-played harmonium, then quietly listen to the clergyman of the "Thames Mission," who has been rowed down here from his floating church, anchored at present in another bay of his liquid parish.

The Royal National Lifeboat Institution had most kindly presented to the *Rob Roy* one of its best lifeboat compasses. The card of this compass floats in a mixture of spirits, so as to steady its oscillations in a boat, and a deft-like lamp alongside will light it up for use by night. Only a sailor knows the peculiar feeling of regard and mystery with which the compass of his craft becomes invested, the companion in past or unknown future perils, his trusty guide over the wide waste of waters and through the night's long blackness.

Having so much iron on board, and so near this wondrous delicate needle, I determined to have the boat "swung" at Greenhithe, where the slack tide allows the largest vessels conveniently to adjust their compasses. This operation consumed a whole day, and a day sufficed for the Russian steamer alongside; but then the time was well bestowed—it was as important to me to steer the *Rob Roy* straight as it could be to any Muscovite that he should sail rightly in his ship of unpronounceable name.*

* "Swinging for the compass" is thus performed. The vessel is moored in the bight at Greenhithe, and by means of warps to certain Government buoys she is placed with her head towards the various points of the compass. The bearing by her compass on board (influenced by the attraction of the iron she carries) is taken accurately by one observer in the vessel, and the true bearing is signalled to him by another observer on shore, who has a compass

While the compass was thus made perfect for use at one end of the boat, her anchors occupied my attention at the other.

It was necessary to carry an anchor heavy enough to hold well in strong tides, in bad weather, and through the long nights, so that I could sleep then without anxiety. On the other hand, the anchor must be also light enough to be weighed and stowed by one man, and this too in that precious twenty seconds of time, when in weighing anchor, the boat, already loosed from the ground but not yet got hold of by the sails, is swept bodily away by the tide, and faces look cross from yachts around, being sure you will collide, as a lubber is bound to do.

After considering the matter of anchors a long time, and poising too the various opinions of numerous advisers, the *Rob Roy* was fitted with a 50-lb. galvanized Trotman anchor and 30 fathoms of chain, and also with a 20-lb. Trotman and a hemp cable.

The operation of anchoring in a new place and that of weighing anchor are certainly among the most testing and risky in a voyage like this, where the circumstances are quite new on each occasion, and where all has to be done by one man.

---

out of reach of the "local attraction" of the vessel. The error in each position due to the local attraction is thus ascertained, and the corrections for these errors are written on a card in a tabulated form, thus:

For	Steer
N.	N. $\frac{1}{4}$ E.
N. by E.	N.N.E.

And so on. A half point looks a small matter on the compass card, but in avoiding a shoal, or in finding a harbour, it makes all the difference.

You sail into a port where in less than a minute you must apprehend by one panoramic glance the positions of twenty vessels, the run of the tide, and set of the wind, and depth of the water; and this not only as these are then existing, but, in imagination, how they will be six hours hence, when the wind has veered, the tide has changed, and the vessels have swung round, or will need room to move away, or new ones will have arrived.

These being the *data*, you have instantly to fix on a spot where there will be water enough to float your craft all night, and yet not so deep as to give extra work next morning; a berth, too, which you can reach as at present sailing, and from which you can start again to-morrow; one where there are no moorings of absent vessels to foul your anchor, and where the wind will not blow right into your sleeping-cabin when the moonlight chills, and where the dust will not blind you from this lime barge, or the blacks begrime you from that coal brig as you spread the yellow butter on your morning tartine.

The interest felt in doing this feat well is increased by seeing how watchfully those who are already berthed will eye the stranger, often speaking by their looks, and always feeling "hope he won't come too near *me*"; while the penalty on failure in the proceeding is heavy and sharp, a smash of your spars, a hole in your side, or a sleepless night, or an hour of cable clearing to-morrow, or all of them; and certainly in addition, the objurgations of every yachtsman within the threatened circle.

Undoubtedly the most unpleasant result of bad management is to have damaged any other man's boat;

and I cannot but mention with the greatest satisfaction, that after so often working my anchors—at least two hundred times—and so many days of sailing in crowded ports and rivers, on no one occasion did the *Rob Roy* even brush the paint off any other vessel.

Not far from my yawl there was moored a fine old frigate, useless now for war, but invaluable for peace— the "*Chichester* Training-ship, for homeless boys of London." It is for a class of lads utterly different from those on the *Worcester*, but they are English boys still, and every Englishman ought to do something for English boys, if he cares for the present or the future of England.

Pale and squalid, thin, heartless, and homeless, they were; but now, ruddy in the river breeze, neat and clean, alert with energy, happy in their wooden home, with a kind captain and smart officers to teach them, life and stir around, fair prospects ahead, and a British seaman's honest livelihood to be earned instead of the miserable puling beggardom of the streets, or the horrid company of the prison cell; which, that they should lie in the path of any child of our land, adrift on the rough tide of time at ten years old, is a glaring shame to the millions of sovereigns in bankers' books, and we shall have to answer heavily if we let it be thus still longer.

The burgee flag of the Canoe Club flew always (white with our paddle across Ↄ C in cipher), and another white flag on the mizen-mast had the yawl's name inscribed. Six other gay colours were used as occasion required. These all being hoisted on a fine bright day, and my voyage really begun, the *Chichester* lads "boyed" the rigging, and gave three ringing cheers as they shouted, "Take these to France, sir!" and the frigate dipped her ensign in salute, my flag lieutenant smartly responding to the compliment as we bade "good-bye."

The Thames to seaward looks different to me every time I float on its noble flood. I have seen it from on board steamers large and small, from an Indiaman's deck, the gunwale of a cutter, and the poop of an iron-clad, as well as from rowboat and canoe, and have penetrated almost every nook and cranny on the water, some of them a dozen times, yet always it is new to see.

Thames river life is a separate world from the land life in houses. The day begins on the water full an hour before sunrise. Cheery voices and hearty faces greet you, and there seems to be no maimed, or sick, or poor. From the simple fact that you are on the river, there is a brotherhood with every sailor. The *mode* is supple as the water, not like the stiff fashion of the land. Ships and shipmen soon become the "people." The other folks on shore are, to be sure, pretty numerous, but then they are ashore. Undoubtedly they are useful to provide for us who are afloat the butter, eggs, and bread they do certainly produce; and we gaze pleasantly on their grassy lawns and bushy trees, and can hear the lark singing on high, and peacocks screaming, and all are very pretty, and we are bound to try to sympathize with people thus pinned to the soil, while we are free in the fine fresh breeze, and glide on the bounding wave. *N.B.*—These very people are all the while regarding *us* with humane pity, as the "poor fellows in that little ship there, cabined, cribbed, confined." Perhaps it is well for all of us that the standpoint of each, be it ever so bleak, becomes to him the centre of creation.

As the country lane has charms for the botanist which will sadly delay one in a summer stroll with such a companion, so to the nautical mind every reach on a full river has a constant flow of incidents quite unnoticed by the landsman. In the crowd of ships around us, no two are quite the same even to look at, nor are they doing the same thing, and there are hundreds passing. What a feast for the eye that hath an appetite! The clink of an anchor-chain, the "Yo-ho!" of a well-timed crew, the flapping of huge sails—I love all these sounds, yes, even the shrill squeal of a pulley thrills my ear with pleasure, and grateful to my nostrils is the odour of tar.

Meanwhile we are sailing on to Sheerness; and no wonder that the *Rob Roy* fixes many a sailor's eye, for the bright sun shines on her new white sails, and her brilliant-coloured flags flutter gladly in the wind as the waves glance and play about her polished mahogany sides, the last and least addition to the yacht fleet of England.

Rounding Garrison Point, at the mouth of the Medway, our anchor is dropped alongside the yacht *Whisper*, where the kind hospitality to the *Rob Roy*, from English, French, and Belgian, at once began, and it ceased only at the end of my voyage.

After our tea and strawberries, and ladies' chat (pleasant ashore and ten times more afloat), the blue-jackets' band on board the Guard-ship gives music, and the moon gives light, and around are the huge old war-hulks, beautiful, though bygone, and all at rest, with a newer, uglier frigate, that has no poetry in her look, but could speak forth loudly, no doubt, with a very heavy broadside, for her thundering salute made all the windows shudder as she steamed in gallantly.

The tide of visitors to my yawl began at Sheerness. Among them I caught a boy and made him grease the mast. His friends were so pleased with their visit, that when the *Rob Roy* came there again months afterwards, they brought me a present of fresh mussels, highly to be esteemed by those who like to eat them—everybody does not; but then was it not grateful to give them thus? and is not gratitude a precious and rare gift to receive?

The internal arrangements of the *Rob Roy* yawl are certainly peculiar, for they were designed for a unique purpose, and as there is no description (at least that I can find) of a yacht specially made for one-man voyages, and proved to be efficient during so long a sail, it may be useful here to describe the inside of the *Rob Roy*. Safety was the first point to be attained, as we have already mentioned, and this was provided for by her breadth of beam (seven feet), her strongly bolted iron kelson, her water-tight compartments, and her double skin, the outer one being of polished Honduras mahogany, and the inner of yellow pine, with canvas between them; also by her strong, firm deck, her under-sized masts and sails, and her lifeboat dingey.

Next we had to consider the capacity for comfort; not for the sake of any luxurious ease which could be expected, but so as to take proper means to preserve health, maintain good spirits, and to economize the energy which would undoubtedly be largely taxed in downright physical muscular work, and which now would be liable any day to yield if overwrought by long-continued anxiety, wakefulness, and exertion.

For this purpose the actual labour bestowed upon maintaining the outward forms of a (partially) civilized life must be a minimum, and the action required in times of risk or danger must be as little encumbered as possible; and as every arrangement came frequently under review, and improvements were well considered in meditative hours, and many were put in practice during a stay at Cowes, where the very best workmen were at command, it may not unreasonably be asserted that for a solitary sailor's yacht the cabin of the *Rob Roy* is at least a very good specimen of the most recent model, and perhaps the best that has been devised as a basis for the next advance.

Although at present I have no radical improvements to suggest upon the general plan, it is, of course, open to the refining experience of others; and I do not apologize for speaking of the fittings of a little boat as if they were mere trifles, because it held only *one* man, when they may in any degree be useful to yachts of larger size, and thus to that noble fleet of roaming craft which renew the nerve and energy of so many Englishmen by a manly and healthful enterprise, opening a whole new element of nature, and nursing a host of loyal seamen to defend our shores.

From the sketch given at p. 45, and one partly in section at p. 58, it will be understood that the *Rob Roy* is fully decked all over except an open well near the stern which is three feet square, and about the same in depth; a strong combing surrounds both the well and the main hatchway, as a protection in a sea.* This

* The after part of the well is rounded at each side, and it is all boarded up. In the middle is a seat on which a large cork cushion can rest, or this may be thrown over as a life-preserver or for a buoy, while the life-belt to be worn round the waist is stowed away under the seat, and an iron basin with a handle is placed alongside it just over the flooring, below which is seen, at p. 58, a wedge of lead-ballast, and in front of this the water-well, where water col-

well or after compartment is separated from the next compartment by a strong bulkhead, sloping forward (p. 58), to give all the room possible for stretching one's limbs and a change of posture, and also so as to form a comfortable sloping back inside in the cabin, while it supports a large soft pillow, the whole being used as a sofa to recline on while reading or writing, or finally being converted into a bolster by lowering it when the crew are piped to bed for the night, or at least such hours of it as the tide and wind may allow for sleep.

Fronting the seat the binnacle hangs with its tender thrilling compass inside, well protected by thick plate glass, and the lamp, which is always ready to be lighted up should darkness need it, for experience has showed me only too plainly that it will not do to postpone any preparation for night, or wind, or hunger, or shoal water, but that you should be always quite prepared for them all.

Above the binnacle is the chart; that is to say a rectangular piece cut out from the larger sheet, and containing all that will be sailed in a day. The other parts, too, of the chart ought to be kept where they are accessible for ready reference.

Rain or the dashing of a wave or two soon softens the paper of the chart, and on one occasion it was so nearly melted away in this manner in a rough sea, that I had

---

lecting from leakage or dashing spray is conveniently reached by the tube of vulcanized india-rubber represented as just in front. This pump hose has a brass union joint on the top, to which we can screw the nozzle of a pump with a copper cylinder (shown at the bottom), or a piston worked by hand (but without any lever), and when in use the cylinder rests obliquely, so that the water will flow out over the combing, and on the deck, and so into the sea.

to learn its lines and figures quickly off by heart, and trust to memory for the rest of the day.

To prevent another time such an awkward state of things, I made a frame with a glass front and movable back, and this allowed each portion of the chart to be placed inside, and to be well protected, an excellent arrangement when your hands are as wet as all other things around, and the ordinary chart would be soaked in five minutes.

The chart frame is also detachable from its place, as it is sometimes necessary to hold it near a lamp at night so as to read the soundings. To aid still further to decipher the chart at night and in dull afternoons, there is a small mounted lens in a leather loop alongside, which has often to be used. The compass* itself is so placed that you can see it well while either sitting or standing up, or when lying at full length on the deck, with the back against a pillow propped by the mizenmast, the bright sun or moon overhead, and a turn or two of the mainsheet cast about your body to keep the sleepy steersman from rolling over into the water, as shown.

This somewhat effeminate but decidedly comfortable attitude in which to keep one's watch on deck, was not invented until farther on in the cruise; and it seems odd that I should so long have continued to sit upright for hours together (wriggling only a little at the constraint) for many a fine day before adopting for a change so obvious a posture, and thus effectually postponing any

* Several important suggestions for the improvement of the lifeboat liquid compass were obtained during my use of it in this voyage, and these have been duly appreciated by the Lifeboat Institution.

sense of weariness even in sailing for a whole day and night. Still it is only for light airs, gentle waves, or in deep rivers, or with long runs on the same tack, that the captain may do his duty while he lies on a sofa. In fresh breezes and rolling seas or in beating to windward with frequent boards, such indulgence is soon cut

Watch on deck

short; and indeed the muscles and energies of the sailor are so braced up by the lively motion and refreshing blasts when there is plenty of wind, that no *ennui* can come; and there is quite enough play of limb and change of position caused by the working of the ship, while he soon learns by practice to steer by the action of any part of his body from head to feet being in contact with the tiller, that delicate and true sensorium of a boat to which all feeling is conveyed.

45

Sometimes I would sit low and out of sight, but with a glance now and then at the compass, while the tiller pressed against my neck. At others I would lie prone on the hatchway with my head upon both hands, and my elbows on the deck, and my foot on the tiller; while, again, every day it was necessary to cook and eat, all the time steering; the most difficult operation of all being to eat a boiled egg comfortably under these conditions, because there is the egg and the spoon, each in a hand, and the salt and the bread, each liable to be capsized with a direful result.

Uncovered and handy for instant use there lies a sharp axe at the bottom of the well, by which any rope may be cut, and a blow may be given to the forelock of an anchor or other refractory point needing instant correction, and near this again is the sounding lead, with its line wound on a stick like that of a boy's kite. I soon found that much the best way to tell the fathoms, especially at night, was to measure the line as it was hauled in by opening my arms to the full stretch of one fathom between my hands.

In two large leather pockets fixed in the well were sundry articles, such as a long knife, cords of various kinds, a foot measure of ivory (best to read off at night), and a good binocular glass by Steward in the Strand.*

Turning now to the left of the seat in the well, we

---

* However good the glass, it is very difficult to make use of it for faint or distant objects on the horizon, and on the whole I found it easier to discern the first dim line of land far off by the unaided eye. A slight mark, that would not be observed while only a short piece of it is seen in the field of view, becomes decidedly manifest if a large scope is seen at once. The binocular glass was very valuable, however, when the words on a buoy, or the colour on the chequers of a beacon had to be deciphered.

open a door about a foot square, hinged so as to fall downwards and thus form a cook's "dresser"; and now the full extent is visible of our kitchen range, at p. 58, or in nautical tongue here is the caboose of the *Rob Roy*.

It is a zinc box with a frame holding a flat copper kettle, a pan in which to heat the tin of preserved meat for our dinner today, and the copper frying-pan in which three eggs will be cooked *sur le plât* for our breakfast tomorrow.

The invaluable Russian lamp * is below this frame, and a spare lamp alongside—a fierce blast it has, and it will be needed if there is bad weather, for then sometimes as a heavy sea is coming the kitchen is hastily closed lest the waves should invade it, but the lamp may still be heard roaring away inside all the same. An iron enamelled plate and a duster complete the furniture of our little scullery, all the rest of the things we started with having been improved out of existence, for simplicity is the heart of invention, as brevity is the soul of wit.

If we desire to get at the tubular wooden flag box that some gay colours may deck our mast in entering a new harbour, this will be found inside the space aft of the caboose; and again, by reaching the arm still further into the hollow behind our seat, it will grasp the *storm mizen*, a strongly made triangular sail, to be used only in untoward hours, and for which we must prepare by lowering the lug mizen, and shifting the halyard, tack, and sheet. Then the *Rob Roy*, with her mainsail and jib reefed, will be under snug canvas.

But now it is bed-time, and the lecture on the furniture of the yawl may be finished some other day.

* See p. 61

CHAPTER II

SHEERNESS is on the whole a tolerable port to land at, that is, as long as you refrain from going ashore. The harbour is interesting and more lively than it appears at first sight, but the streets and shops are just the reverse.

The *Rob Roy* ran into this harbour seven or eight times during her cruise, and there was always "something going on." The anchorage on the south of the pier is in mud of deep black colour, but not such good holding ground as it would seem to be, and then what comes up on the anchor runs like black paint upon your deck, and needs a good scrubbing to get rid of it from each palm of the anchor. Even after all seems to be cleared away thoroughly, there may be a piece only the size of a nut, but perverse enough to fasten upon the white creamy folds of your jib newly washed out, and then the inky stain will be an eyesore for days, until, for peace of mind, the sail must be scrubbed again. Trifles these are to the yachtsman who can leave all that to his crew, who sees only *results*, but when the captain alone is the crew, the realities of sea life must be endured as well as enjoyed, and yet surely he is the one to enjoy most keenly the luxury of a white spotless sail whose own hands have made it so.

If any sailor henceforth has me for his captain, and he has to "tidy up" my yacht, he may be sure of having a very considerate if not indulgent master—"Governor," of course, I mean, for there are no "masters" any longer now, they are all promoted to the rank of "Governor."

And the reason I should be considerate is that until you do it all yourself you cannot have any idea of the innumerable *minutiæ* to be attended to in the proper care of a yacht. Mine, indeed, was in miniature; but the number of little things was still great, though each little thing was more little. On the whole, we should say that a yacht's crew, even in port, have full employment for all their working hours if the hull, spars, sails, ropes, and boats, besides the cabin and stores, are always kept in that condition of order, neatness, cleanliness, readiness, and repair which ought to be little short of perfection when regarded with a critical eye.

In like manner as you drive out in a carriage and return, and the carriage and horses disappear into the stables for hours of careful work by the men who are there, so may the day's sail in a yacht involve a whole series of operations on board afterwards. Inattention to these in the extreme can be observed in the boats of fishermen, and attention in the extreme in the perfect vessels of the Royal Squadron; but even a very reasonable amount of smartness requires a large expenditure of labour which will not be effectual if it be hurried, and which is, of course, worse than useless if it is done by inferior hands.

In perfect trim and "ship shape" now, we loosed from Sheerness, to continue the sail eastwards, and with a leading breeze and a lovely morning. This part of the Thames is about the best conjunction of river and sea one could find, with land easily sighted on both sides, yet fine salt waves, porpoises, and other attributes of the sea, and buoys, and beacons, and lightships to be attended to, and a definite line of course determined on and followed by compass. A gale here is not to be trifled with, though in fine weather you may pass it safely in a mere cockle-shell, and the last time I had sailed here alone it was in an open boat, just ten feet long inside. Still the whole day may be summed up now, as it was in the log of the *Rob Roy*, "Fine run to Margate"; the pleasures of it were just the same as so often afterwards were met, enjoyed, and thanked for, but which might be tedious to relate even once.

The harbour here dries bare at low tide, and as seventeen years had elapsed since we had sailed into it, this bad habit of the harbour was forgotten, but more years than that may pass before it will be forgotten again, for as evening came, and the water ebbed, and I reclined unharnessed in the cabin, reading intently, there suddenly came a rude bumping shove upwards as from below, and then another—the *Rob Roy* had grounded. Soon there was a swaying this way and that, as if yet undecided, and at length a positive heel over to *that*; the whole of my little world within being canted to half a right angle, and a ridiculous distortion of every single thing in my bedroom was the result. The humiliating sensation of being aground on hard un-romantic mud is tempered by the ludicrous crooked appearance of the contents of your cabin, and by the absurd sensation of sleeping in a corner with everything askance except the lamp flame, which, because it burns upright, looks most awry of all, and incongruously flares on the spout of the teapot in your pantry.

And why this *bouleversement* of all things? Because I

had omitted to bring a pair of legs with me, for a boat cannot stand upright on shore without legs any more than an animal.

Next time the *Rob Roy* came to Margate we made one powerful leg for her by lashing the two oars to the iron shroud, and took infinite pains to incline the boat over to that side, so as to be turned away from the wind and screened from the tide, and I therefore weighted her down by placing the dingey and heavy anchor on the lee gunwale, and then with misplaced contentment proceeded to cook my dinner. At a solemn pause in the repast, the yawl, without other warning than a loud splash, perversely turned over to the wrong side, with deck to sea and wind, and every single thing exactly the contrary of what was proper. I had just time to plunge my hissing spirit-lamp into the sea, and thus to prevent the cry of "Ship on fire!" but had not time to put out my cabin-lamp, and this instantly bore its flame provokingly upright against the thick glass of the aneroid barometer, which duly told its fate by three sonorous "crinks", and at once three starred cracks shot through its crystal front.

The former experience of the night as spent when one is thus arbitrarily "inclined to sleep," made me wish to get ashore; but this idea was stifled partly by pride, and partly by the fact that there was not water enough to enable me to go ashore in a boat, and yet there was too much water besides soft mud to make it at all pleasant to set off and wade to bed. The recovery from this unwholesome state of things, with all the world askew, was equally notable, for when the tide rose again, in the late midnight hours, the sea-dreams of disturbed slumber were arrested by a gentle nudge, and then by a more decided heaving up of one's bed in the dark, until at last it came level again as the boat floated, and all the things that were right when she was wrong turned over now at wrong angles, because the boat had righted.*

An excellent cure for all such little mishaps is to "imagine it is to-morrow morning," for in the morning one is sure to forget all the night's troubles; and so with the fiery rising sun on the sails we are floating out to sea.

In such a sunny day the North Foreland is a very comfortable-looking cliff, with pleasant country-houses on the top, and cornfields growing round the lighthouse. Next there is Ramsgate, and then Dover pier. But now, and in weather like this, will be a proper occasion to practise manœuvres which will certainly have to be performed in bad times, so we stretched away out to the Goodwin Sands, where one is nearly always sure to find a sea running, and for several hours we worked assiduously at reefing the sails, and getting the little dingey out of the cabin and into the water, and vice versa.

At least a short trial of my yacht in the Thames would have been advisable before starting on a long voyage, but as this was not possible now, it was of invaluable benefit to spend an afternoon at drill on the Goodwin; rightly assured that success in this journey could not be expected haphazard, but might be hoped for after the *practice in daylight and fine weather of what had to be done afterwards in rough water and darkness.*

* In yet another, the fourth visit to this stupid shallow harbour (one of the most unpleasant to lie in anywhere), I fixed an oar out at each side as a leg, and could scarcely get rest from the fear that one or other of my beautiful oars would be snapped as they bent and groaned with remonstrances against supporting several tons of weight in the capacity of a wooden leg.

By this time, just a week in the *Rob Roy*, the little craft seemed quite an old friend. Her many virtues and her few faults were being found out. The happy life aboard had almost enchained me, but still I left the yawl at Dover, and ran up to London for the annual inspection of the London Scottish Volunteers; and having led his fine company of kilted Riflemen through Hyde Park, the Captain sheathed his claymore to handle the tiller again, eager for the voyage.

The new rough hairy ropes had chafed my hands abundantly, and they were red and black, and blistered, and swollen, and variously adorned by cuts, and bruises, and scars. When shall I ever get gloves on again, or be fit to appear at a dinner-table? These wounds, however, had taught me this lesson, "Do every act deliberately. Hasty smartness is slowest. When each single thing from morning to night has to be done by your own fingers, save them from bruises and chafes. Nothing is worse spent than needless muscular action. You will want every atom you have some day or other this week. Husband vital force."

The *Sappho* schooner was at Dover, and her owner, Mr. Lawton, one of the Canoe Club, took leave of the *Rob Roy*, and sailed away to Iceland, while I started for Boulogne in the dawn, when all the scene around looked like a woodcut, pale and colourless, as I cooked hot breakfast at five o'clock. Nothing particular happened in this voyage across the Channel. It was simply a very pleasant sail, in a very fine day, and in a good little boat. The sight of both shores at once, when you are in the widest part of a passage, deprives it immediately of the romance and interest of being entirely out of sight of land and ships, and all else but water, and so there is absent that deeper stir of feeling which powerfully seized me in the wider traverse afterwards from Havre to Cowes.

Indeed, when you know the under-water geography of the channel near Dover, it is impossible not to feel that you are sailing over shallow waves; for though they seem to be deep and grand enough from Dover Castle or the Boulogne heights, the whole way might almost be spanned by piers and arches, and if you wished to walk over dry shod at the low spring-tide, you need only lay from shore to shore a twenty miles' slice of undulated ground cut from the environs of London. The cellars of the houses would be at the bottom of the sea, but the chimney-pots would still be above it for stepping-stones.

The wind fell as we neared France, and a fog came on, and the tide carried us off in a wrong direction north to Cape Grisnez, where I anchored with twenty fathoms, to wait for the reflux six or seven hours. Often as we had to do the same thing in after days, there was always constant employment for every hour of a long stoppage like this, with a well-furnished tool-box, and a busy mind, ever making additions, experiments, improvements, and with books to read. Not one single moment of the voyage ever hung heavy in the *Rob Roy*.

Trying to get into Boulogne at low water was an unprepared attempt, and met its due reward; for the thing had to be done without the benefit of my "Pilot-book," which had been put away with such exceeding care, that now it could not anywhere be found—not after several rigorous searches all over the boat. Finally, concluding that I must have taken the book to

London by mistake, we had to trust to nature's light and go ahead. This does well enough for a canoe, but not for the sailing-boat, which, if once aground, and with a sea running, it would be utterly out of the power of one man to save.*

In encountering the first roller off the pier at Boulogne, she thumped the ground heavily. At the second, again, the masts quivered, and all the bottles rattled in my cellar. Instant decision turned her round from the third roller, and so, after bumping the ground twice again in the retreat, we put out to sea, anchored, and got out the dingey, half-ashamed to be discomfited thus at the very first French port. After an hour or two spent in the dark, carefully sounding to discover the proper channel, and to get it well into my head, the anchor was weighed, and we entered in a poor sort of triumph about midnight, slowly ascending the long harbour, but looking in vain for a proper berth. All was quiet, every one seemed to be in bed, until I came to the sluices at the end, which just then opened, and the rush of foaming water from these bore me back again in the most helpless plight, until I anchored near the well-known "Etablissement," furled sails, rigged up hatch, and soon dropped fast asleep.

Now there is a peculiarity of the French ports which we may mention here once for all, but it applies to every one of them, and has to be seriously considered in all your calculations as a sailing-master.

They are quiet enough up to a certain time of night, but as the tide serves, the whole port awakes, all the

---

* I had lessened her ton and a half of iron ballast by leaving two hundredweight on Dover quay; good advice agreeing with my own opinion that the *Rob Roy* was needlessly stiff.

fishing-vessels get ready to start. The quays become vocal with shouts, yells, calls, whistles, and the most stupid din and hubbub confounds the night, utterly destructive of sleep. This chorus was in full cry about 2 a.m. Soon great luggers came splashing along with shrieks from the crews, and sails flapping, chains rattling, spars knocking about, as if a tempest were in rage. Several of these lubberly craft smashed against the pier, and the men screamed more wildly, and at length one larger and more inebriated than all the rest, dashed in among the small boats where the *Rob Roy* slept, and swooping down on the poor little yawl, then wrapt in calm repose, she heeled us over on our beam-ends, and after fastening her clumsy, rusty anchor in my mizen shrouds (which were of iron, and declined to snap), she bore me and my boat away far off, igno-miniously, stern foremost.

Certainly this was by no means a pleasant foretaste of what might be expected in the numerous other ports we were to enter, and, at any rate, that night's sleep was gone. But in a voyage of this sort a night's sleep must be resigned readily, and the loss is easily borne by trying to forget it, which indeed you soon do when the sun rises, and a good cup of tea has been quaffed, or, if that will not suffice, then another.

Vigorous health is at the bottom of the enthusiastic enjoyment of yachting; but in a common sailor's life sleep is not a regular thing as we have it on shore, and perhaps that staid glazy and sedate-looking eye, which a hard-worked seaman usually has, is really caused by broken slumber. He is never completely awake, but he is never entirely asleep.

Boulogne is a much more agreeable place to reside at

than one might suppose from merely passing through it. Once I spent a month there, and found plenty to see and to do. Good walks, hotels, churches, and swimming-baths. The river to row in, the reading-room to sit in, the cliffs to climb, and the sands to see.

At Dover the dock-people had generously charged me "nil" for dues. I had letters for France from the highest authorities to pass the *Rob Roy* as an article entered for the Paris Exhibition; and when the *douane* and police functionaries came in proper state at Boulogne to appraise her value, and to fill up the numerous forms, certificates, schedules, and other columned documents, I had hours of walking to perform, and most courteous and tedious attention to endure, and then paid for sanitary dues, "two sous per ton," that was threepence. Finally, there was this insurmountable difficulty, that though all my ship's papers were *en règle*, they must be signed "by two persons on board," so I offered to sign first as captain and then as cook. They never troubled me again in any other port, probably thinking the boat too small to have come from a foreign harbour. In France the law of their paternal Government prevents any Frenchman from sailing thus alone.

The sun warmed a fine fresh breeze from the N.E. as we coasted from Boulogne, and to sail with it was a luxury all day. The first pleasure was the morning ablution, either by a wholesale dip under the waves, or a more particular toilette if the *Rob Roy* was then in full sail.

To effect this we push the hatch forward, and open the interior of the boat. If the water we float on is clean (whether it be salt or fresh) we dip the tin basin at once, but if we are in a muddy river or doubtful harbour we must draw from our zinc water tank, which holds water for one week. This tank is concealed by the figure of the cook kneeling in the sketch, but it is next to my large portmanteau in the lower shelf.

A large hole in the top of the tank allows it to be filled at intervals through a tun-dish, while a long vulcanized

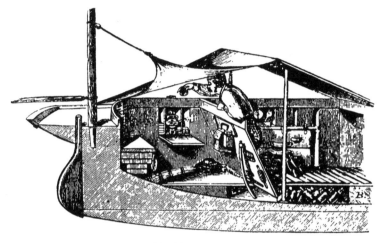

Cooking in rain

tube through the cork to the bottom has an end hanging over. When I wish to draw water it is done by applying the mouth for a moment with suction, and the clear stream then flows by siphon action into a strong tin can of about eight inches cube, which holds fresh water for one day. By means of this tube, the end of which hangs within an inch or two of my face when in bed, I can drink a cool draught at night without trouble or chance of spilling a drop. On the tank top is soap, and also a clean towel, which to-morrow will be degraded into a duster, and "relegated", the newspapers would say, to the kitchen, whence it will again be promoted backwards over the bulkhead to the washing-bag. This you see is the red-tape order of dealing with towels on board the *Rob Roy*.

On the left shelf of the cabin we find two boxes of japanned tin each about eighteen inches by six inches wide, as shown in the woodcut. Below the shelf is a portmanteau full of clothes. One of the boxes holds "Dressing," another "Reading and writing." The aneroid barometer and my watch are seen suspended alongside. The boxes on the other side are marked "Tools" and "Eating", while the pantry is beside them, with teapot, cup (saucer discarded), and tumbler, and a tray holding knife and fork, spoons, salt in a snuff-box (far the best cellar after trials of many), pepper (coarse, or it is blown away), mustard, corkscrew, and lever-knife for preserved meat tins, &c., &c.*

The north coast of France from Boulogne to Havre is well lighted at night, but the navigation is dangerous on account of the numerous shoals and the tortuous currents and tides. For about the first half of the distance the shores are low, and the water, even far out, is shallow. Afterwards the land rises to huge red cliffs, rugged and steep sometimes for miles, without any opening.

The real matter of importance, however, in coasting here is the direction of the wind. Had it been unfavourable, that is S.W., and with the fogs and sea

* The relative positions of all these articles had been maturely considered and carefully arranged, and they were much approved by the most experienced and critical of the many hundred visitors who inspected the *Rob Roy*.

which that wind brings, it would have been a serious delay to me—perhaps, indeed, a stopper on my voyage —seeing that I must sometimes enter a port at night so as to sleep in peace, for that could scarcely be pleasantly done if anchored ten miles from land, and with no one awake to keep a look-out. Fortunately we had good weather on the worst parts of the French coast, and my stormy days were yet to come.

CHAPTER III

AFTER a wash and morning prayers the crew are piped
to breakfast, so we must now turn to the kitchen, which
after constant use some hundred times I cannot but
feel is the most successful "hit" in the whole equipment.

Much thought and many experiments were bestowed
on this subject, because, first, it was well known that
the hard and uneven strain of bone, muscle, and energy
in a voyage of this sort needs to be maintained by
generous diet, that cold feeding is a delusion after a
few days of it, and that the whole affair would fail, or at
any rate, enjoyment of the trip would cease, unless the
Rob Roy had a caboose, easy to work, speedy in result,
and capable of being used in rain, wind, and rough
weather, and by night as well as by day.

Of course, all stoves with coal or coke, or similar fuel
were out of the question, being hard to light, dusty
when lighted, and dirty to clean. Various spirit lamps,
Etnas, Magic stoves, Soyers, and others, were examined
and tried, and all were defective in grand points.

The Russian lamp used by the Alpine climber who
occupies the responsible post of "Cook of the Canoe
Club," was found far superior to all these. This lamp
is less than three inches each way, and has no wick,
but acts after the manner of a blow pipe. In two
minutes after lighting it pours forth a vehement flame
about a foot in height, which with a warming heat

boils two large cups full in my flat copper kettle in five minutes, or a can of preserved meat in six minutes.*

While the kettle is boiling we bring forward the box marked "Eating," take the loaf of bread out of its macintosh swathing, prepare the egg pan with two eggs, the tea-pot, and put sugar into the tea-cup, and a spoonful of preserved milk (Amey's is most convenient, being in powder; but Borden's, in a kind of paste, is most agreeable); lastly, we overhaul the butter tin and pot of marmalade or anchovies.

The healthful relish with which a plain hot breakfast of this sort is consumed with the fresh air all round, and the sun athwart the east, and the waves dancing while the boat sails merrily all the time, is enhanced by the pleasure of steering and buttering bread, and holding a hot egg and a tea-cup, all at once.

Then, again, there is the satisfaction of doing all this without giving needless trouble in cleaning up, for every whit of that work, too, is to be yours. A crumb must not fall in the boat, because you will have to stoop down afterwards and pick it up, seeing that whatever happens, one thing is insisted on—"the *Rob Roy* shall be always smart and clean."

All the breakfast things are cleared away and put by, each into its proper place, and a general "mop up" has effaced the scene from our deck, but we can still take a look below and notice what is to be seen.

Some of the articles chiefly important in the well of

* In the sketch at page 58, the cook of the *Rob Roy* is represented as he works when rain compels him to shelter himself in the cabin under a tarpaulin, and the hatch inclined upwards. But usually —indeed, always but on two occasions—he sat in the well while he tended the caboose.

our boat have been already described, but only those on the left of the steersman sitting. Now, turning to the right we find a water-tight door, like that on the opposite side, to be opened by folding down, and it reveals to us, first the "Bread store," a fourpenny loaf wrapped in macintosh, which makes the best of table-cloths, as it may be laid on a wet deck, and can be washed and dried again speedily; next there is a butter keg (as in the coolest place), and a box of biscuits, and a flask of rum—the "Storm supply"—only to be drawn upon when things of air and sea are in such state that to open the main hatch would be questionable prudence.

Here are, also, ropes, blocks, and purchases, as well as a fender, not to keep coals on the hearth, but to keep the mahogany sides of the *Rob Roy* safe from the rude jostlings of other craft coming alongside. Above these odds and ends is the "Spirit room," a strong reservoir made of zinc, with a tap and screw plug, and internal division, not to be rendered intelligible by mere description here, but of important use, as from hence there is served out, two or three times daily, the fuel which is to cook for the whole crew. One gallon of the methylated spirits, costing four shillings and sixpence, will suffice for this during six weeks.

Above the spirit room will be found a blue light to be used in case of distress, and a box of candles, so that we may be enabled to rig up the mast-light if darkness comes when it will not do to open the cabin. This ship-light is therefore carried here. It is an article of some importance, having to be strong and substantial, easily suspended and taken down, and one that can be trusted to show a good steady light for at least eight hours, however roughly it may be tossed about when you are fast asleep below, in the full confidence that nobody who sees your mast-light will run his great iron bows over your little mahogany bed-room. Yet I fear it does not do to examine into the grounds for any such confidence. Many vessels sail about in the dark without any lights whatever to warn one of their approach, and not a few boats, even with proper lights in them, are accidentally run over and sunk in the River Thames; while out at sea, and in dark drizzly rain or fog, it is more than can be expected of human nature that a "look-out man" should peer into the thick blackness for an hour together, with the rain blinding him, and the spray splash smarting his eyes, and when already he has looked for fifty-nine minutes without anything whatever to see. It is in that last minute, perhaps, that the poor little hatch-boat has come near, with the old man and a boy, its scanty crew, both of them nodding asleep after long watches, and their boat-light swinging in the swell. There is a splash, a crash, and a spluttering, and the affair is over, and the dark is only the dark again. Nobody on the steamer knows that anything has occurred, and only the fishermen to-morrow on some neighbouring bank will see a broken hull, floating sideways, near some tangled nets.

I fully believe that more care is taken for the lives of others by sailors at sea than in most cases on land where equal risks are run; but there are dangers on the waves, as well as on the hills, the roads, and even in the streets, which no foresight can anticipate, and no precaution can avert.

The principal danger of a coasting voyage, sailing alone, is that of being run down, especially on the thickly traversed English coast, and at night.

As for the important question concerning the "rule of the road" at sea, which is every now and then raised, discussed, and then forgotten again after some collision on a crowded river in open day has frightened us into a proper desire to prevent such catastrophes, it appears to me that no rule whatever could possibly be laid down for even general obedience under such circumstances, without causing in its very observance more collisions than it would avert, unless the traffic in the river were to be virtually arrested.

On land the "rule of the road" is well enough on a *road*, where vehicles are moving in one of two directions, but how would it do if it were to be insisted upon at the place where two streets cross? Now the Thames and other populous rivers are at times as much blocked and crowded by the craft that sail and steam on the water as the crossing at Ludgate Hill is by vehicles at three o'clock, that is, considering fairly the relative sizes of the objects in motion, and the width of the path they must take, their means of stopping or steering, and, above all, the great additional forces on the water which cannot be arrested—*wind* and *tide*. And at this crossing the traffic has to be regulated by policemen, that is, not by a *rule* for the drivers but by an external arbitrary director.

The wonderful dexterity of the cabmen, carmen, and coachmen of London is less wonderful than that of the men who guide the barges, brigs, and steamers on the Thames, and it is perfectly amazing that huge masses weighing thousands of tons, and bristling with masts and spars, and rugged wheels projecting, should be every day led over miles of water in dense crowds, round crooked points, along narrow guts, and over hidden shoals, while gusts from above, and whirling eddies below, are all conspiring to confuse the clearest head, to baffle the strongest arm, and to huddle up the whole mass into a general wreck.

Consider what would be the result in the Strand if no pedestrian could stop his progress within three yards, but by anchoring to a lamp-post, and even then swinging round with force. Why, there would be scarcely a coal-heaver who would not be whitened by collision with some baker's boy. Ladies in full sail would be run down, and dandies would be sunk by the dozen.

The fact is, that vessels on the wide sea are like travellers on a broad plain and not on a road at all, and the two cases do not admit of being dealt with by the same rule, and it is not wonderful that there should be many collisions in the open sea while there are so few in the Thames, the water street of the world. We may learn some lessons from land for safe traffic on water. The cabman who "pulls up" is sure to signal first with his whip to the omnibus astern of him, and the coachman who means to cross to the "wrong side" never does so without a warning to those he is bearing down upon. What is most wanted, then, on the open water, is some ready, sure, and costless signal, to say, "I am going *that* way" (right or left); for nearly all collisions at sea are caused by one ship not being able to know what the other is going to do.*

This is my thought on the matter after many thoughts

* I have read numerous books, pamphlets, and discussions on this subject, some of which are wonderfully clear in explaining what is perfectly easy to understand, while they are exceedingly ingenious in overlooking the only difficulty, which is, how a man on one vessel is to know whither another vessel is steering.

and some experience: meantime while we have ate, and talked and thought, our yawl has slipped over six miles of sea, and we must rouse up from a reverie to scan the changing picture.

Glance at the barometer—note the time. Trim the sails, and bear away to that pretty fleet of fishing-boats bobbing up and down as they trail their nets, or the men gather in the glittering fish, and munch their rude breakfasts, tediously heated by smoky stoves, while they gaze on the white-sailed stranger, and mumble among themselves as to what in the world *he* can be. The sun mounts and the breeze presses till we are at the bay of the Somme, with its shifting sands, its incomprehensible currents, and its low and treacherous coast, buoyed and beaconed enough to puzzle you right into the shoals. The yacht, with my friend S—— in her, bound for Paris, has just been wrecked on that bank near Cayeux —unpleasant news now—and there is St. Valery, from whence King William the Conqueror sailed with his fleet for England, as may be seen on the curious tapestry at Bayeux worked by his Queen's hands, and still almost as fresh as then. I never saw a place appear so differently from sea and from land as this strange port, so I ran in just to reconnoitre, and spent some hours with chart, compass, lead-line, and Pilot-book, trying my best to make out the currents, but all to no purpose, except to conclude that a voyage along this coast in bad weather would be madness, unless with a man to help.

But nearly all this part of the French coast is awkward ground to be caught in, especially where there are shifting or sinking sands, for if the vessel touches these, the tide stream instantly sucks the sand from under one side, while it piles it up on the other, and thus the hull is gradually worked in with a ridge on each side, and cannot be slewed off, but is liable to be wrecked forthwith. It was interesting to read here the account of this coast given by my Pilot-book, which had at last been dug out of its hiding-place. The reader need not peruse this official statement, but to justify my remarks on the dangers it is given below in a note.*

* "*Caution.*—During strong winds between W.S.W., round westerly, and N.N.W., the coast to the eastward of Ailly Point is dangerous to be on, and shipwrecks are of frequent occurrence; vessels therefore of every description at that period should keep a good offing, and when obliged to approach it, must do so with great caution; for although the general mass of the above banks appear to be stationary, yet great attention must be paid to the lead, and in observing the confused state of the sea in the various eddies, so as to guard against suddenly meeting with dangers which may be of recent formation. The lights for the purpose of pointing out the position of the headlands and dangers between Capes Antifer and Gris-Nez at night, are so disposed, that in clear weather two can always be seen at a time, and the greater number of the harbours have one or more tide-lights shown during the time the harbour can be entered.

"It is important to notice that along the coast, between Cape de la Hève and the town of Ault (a space of 67 miles), the wind, when it blows in a direction perpendicular, or nearly so, to the direction of the coast, is reflected by the high cliffs, neutralizing in great measure its original action to a certain extent in the offing, depending upon the strength of the wind. It follows from this, that a zone is formed off the coast and parallel to it (except in front of the wide valleys, where the direct wind meets with no obstacle), where the wind is light, the sea much agitated, and the waves run towards the shore. On the contrary, when the wind forms an acute angle with the coast, the reflected wind contributes to increase the direct wind near the shore."

CHAPTER IV

THE aneroid barometer in my cabin pointed to "set fair" for many a day, and just, too, when we required it most to be fine, that is along the French coast. Had the *Rob Roy* encountered here the sort of weather she met with afterwards on the south coast of England, we feel quite assured she must have been wrecked ashore or driven out to sea for a miserable time.

So it was best to keep moving on while fine weather lasted, for there was no knowing when this might change, even with the wind as now in the good N.E. The Pilot-book says, upon this (and pray listen to so good an authority—my only one to consult with), "Gales from N. to N.E. are also violent, but they usually last only from 24 to 36 hours, and the wind does not shift as it does with those from the westward. They cause a heavy sea on the flood stream, and during their continuance the French coast is covered with a white fog, which has the appearance of smoke. This is also the case with all easterly winds, which are sometimes of long duration, and blow with great force."

In the evening, as a sort of practical comment on the text above, there was a sudden fall of the wind, and then a loud peal of thunder. Alert in a moment, we noticed, far away in the offing, the fishing-boats dip their sails and reef them, so we knew there would soon be a blow, and we resolved to reef, too, and just in time. My life-belt,* therefore, was at once strapped on, and two reefs put in the mainsail, and one in the jib, and the storm mizen was set, all in regular order, when up sprung a fine west breeze, just as we were opposite Treport, a pretty little bathing town under some cliffs, where my night-quarters were to be.

The book already referred to gave a rather serious account of the difficulties of entering Treport, its shingle bar, and the high seas on it, and the cross tide and exceedingly narrow entrance; but in an hour more the *Rob Roy* had come close to all these things, and rose and fell on the rollers chasing each other ashore.

The points to be kept in line for entering the harbour were all clearly set forth in the book, and the signals on the pier were all faultlessly given, while a crowd gradually collected to see the little boat run in, or be smashed, and it was rather exciting to feel that one bump on the bar with such a sea, and—in two minutes the yawl would be a helpless wreck.

Among the spectators, the only one who did not hold

---

* As a precaution, I always put on the life-belt when I had to reef, as one is liable then to be jerked overboard; also in strong winds when we ran before them, because in case of getting overboard then, it would be difficult to catch the yawl by swimming; also at night when sailing, or when sleeping on deck, as one might then be suddenly run down. But with all this prudence it happened that on each of the three occasions when I did fall into the water, I had not the life-belt on. The Lifeboat Institution had presented to me one of their life-jackets—an invaluable companion if a long immersion in the water is to be undergone. But for convenience in working the ropes and sails I was content to use the less bulky life-belt. It is conveniently arranged, and you soon forget it as an encumbrance. Indeed, on one occasion I walked up to a house without recollecting that my life-belt was upon me when ashore!

his hat on against the wind, was an extraordinary personage who capered about shouting. Long curly hair
waved over his face; his dress was hung round with
corks and tassels; he swung a long life-line round his
head, and screamed at me words which were, of course,
utterly lost in the breeze. This dancing dervish was the
"life-saver," marine preserver, and general bore of the
occasion, and he seemed unduly annoyed to see me
profoundly deaf to his noise as I stood on the after-deck
to get a wider view, holding on by the mizen-mast,
steering with my feet, and surveying the entrance with
my glass. All the people ran alongside as the *Rob Roy*
glided past the pier and smoothly berthed upon a great
mud bank exactly as desired, and then I apologized to
the quaint Frenchman, saying that I could not answer
him before, for really I had enough to do to steer
my boat, at which all the rest laughed heartily—but we
made it up next day, and the dervish and *Rob Roy* were
good friends again.

Here we found the *Onyx*, an English-built yacht, but
owned by M. Charles, one of the few Frenchmen to be
found who really seems to *like* yachting; plenty of them
affect it.

He was enthusiastic in his hospitality, and I rested
there next day, meeting also an interesting youth, an
eager sailor, but who took sea trips for his health, and
drove from some Royal Château to embark and freshen
the colour in his delicate face, so pale with languor.
We could not but feel and express a deep sympathy
with one who loved the sea, but whose pallid looks were
in such contrast to the rough brown hue and redundant
health enjoyed so long by myself.

All was ataunt again, and then the two yachts

started in company for a run to Dieppe, which is only about thirteen miles distant. We came upon a nest of twelve English yachts, all in the basin of this port, so my French comrade spent the rest of his time gazing at their beauty, their strength, their cleanliness, and that unnamed quality which distinguishes English yachts and English houses, a certain fitness for their special purpose. These graceful creatures (is it possible that a fine yacht can be counted as an inanimate thing?) reclined on the muddy bosom of the basin, but I would not put the *Rob Roy* there, it seemed so pent up and torpid a life, and with the curious always gazing down from the lofty quay right into your cabin, especially as next day I wished to have a quiet Sunday.

Instead of a peaceful day of rest the Sunday at Dieppe was unusually bustling from morning to night, for it was the *Fête Dieu* there. The streets were dressed in gala, and strewed with green herbs, while along the shop fronts was a broad festooned stripe of white calico, set off by roses here and there; the shipping, too, was decked in flag array, and guns, bells, and trombones ushered a long procession of schools and soldiers, and young people coming from their "first communion," who with their priests, and banners, and relics, halted round temporary altars in the open air, to recite and chant, while a vast crowd followed to gaze.

In a similar procession at St. Cloud, one division of the moving host was of the tiniest little children, down to the lowest age that could manage to toddle along with the hand of a mother or sister to help, and the leader of them all was a chubby little boy, with no headgear in the hot sun but his curly hair, and with his arms and body all bare, except where a lambskin hung across. He carried a blue cross, too, and the pretty child looked bewildered enough. Some thought he was John the Baptist, many more pronounced it a *sottise*.

In the canoe voyages of the two preceding summers, I had found much pleasure and interest in carrying a supply of books, pictures, and periodicals, and illustrated stories in various languages, which were given as occasion admitted to all sorts of people, and everywhere accepted with thanks, so that we could only regret the limit imposed on the number to be carried in a canoe, where every ounce of weight added to the muscular toil.

Relieved now from this restriction, the *Rob Roy* yawl was able to load several boxes of this literary cargo, most of them kindly granted for the special purpose of her voyage.

These presents were given away from day to day, and especially on Sunday afternoons, among the sailors and water-population wherever the *Rob Roy* roved. Thousands of seamen can read, and have time, but no books. Bargees lolling about, or prone in the sun, eagerly began a "Pilgrim's Progress" when thus presented, and sometimes went on reading for hours. Fishermen came off in boats to ask for them, policemen and soldiers, too, begged for a book, and then asked for another for a "child at school." Smart yachtsmen were most grateful of all, and some even offered to pay for them; the navvies, lock-keepers, ferrymen, watermen, porters, dock-men, and guard-men of lighthouses, piers, and hulks, as well as many a Royal Navy blue-jacket, gratefully accepted these little souvenirs with every appearance of gratitude.

The distribution of these was thus no labour, but a constant pleasure to me. Permanent and positive good may have been done by the reading of their contents; at any rate, they opened up conversation, gave scope to courteous intercourse, often leading to kinder interest. They opened to me many new scenes of life, and some with darker passages and sorrowful groups in the evident but untold background. They were, in fact, the speediest possible introductions by which to meet at once with large bodies of fellow-men too much unknown to us, therefore forgotten, and then despised. The strata of society are not to be all crushed into a pulpy mass, but a wholesome mingling betimes does good, both to the heavy dregs below and to the *crême* on the very top.

Thus encouraged, we launch the little dingey on Sunday for three or four hours' rowing, and with a large leather bag well filled at starting, but empty on its return; and instead of its contents we bring back in our memory a whole series of tales, characters, and incidents of water-craft life, some tragic, others comic, many "hum-drum" enough, but still instructive, suggestive, branching out into hidden lives one would like to draw forth, and telling sorrows that are softened by being told. Of the French crews I began with here, not one of the first few could even read, while five or six English steamboats took books for all their men. On a preceding Sunday (at Erith), I did not meet one man, even a bargee, who could not read, and all up the Seine only one in this predicament. Truly there is a sea-mission yet to be worked. Good news was told on the water long ago, and by the Great Preacher from a boat.

. . . .

74

CHAPTER V

So much for Sunday thoughts; but after the day had ended, there happened to me an absurd misery, of the kind considered to be comical, and so beyond sympathy, but which must be told, and it happened thus:—

The little yawl being anchored in the harbour had also a long rope to the quay, and by this I could draw her near the foot of an upright ladder of iron bars fixed in the stones of the quay wall, an ordinary plan of access in such cases. The pier-man promised faithfully to watch my boat as the tide sunk (it was every moment more and more under his very nose), and so to haul her about that she should not "ground" before my return; yet, when I came back at night, her keel had sunk and sunk until it reached the bottom, so she could not be moved with all our pulling. Moreover, the tide had gone out so far as to prevent any boat at all from coming to the dock wall round the harbour. I tried to amuse myself for an hour while the tide might rise; but at length, impatient and sleepy and ready for bed, to be off to-morrow at break of day, I determined to get on board at once somehow or other.

Descending then by the iron bars until I reached the last of them, I swung myself on the slack of the strong cable hanging from above (and attached at the other end to my yawl), and which the man received strict orders to "haul taut" at the critical moment. Alas!

75

in his clumsy hands the effect intended was exactly reversed; the rope was gently loosened, and I subsided in the most undignified, inevitable, and provokingly cool manner, quietly into the water at 10.30 p.m. However, there was no use in grumbling, so I spluttered and laughed, and then went to bed.

Long before sunrise the *Rob Roy* was creeping out of the harbour of Dieppe against the strong wind at that point dead ahead; but I took the tow-line thrown down from the quay by some sturdy fishwives, who will readily tug a boat to the pier head for a franc or two, and thus save a good half-hour of tedious rowing against wind and tide. This rope was of a deep black colour, very fine, thin, and yet strong. There was no time to find out what it was made of, but it seemed to be plaited of human hair. As I was aft in my boat and steering, the line suddenly slipped and disappeared, and the *Rob Roy* was in great danger of going adrift on the other pier head, but the excellent dames speedily regained their long black

A tumble in

tress, and coiled it and threw it to me again with great dexterity; and soon all was put right, and the sails were up, and the line cast off, and we plunged along in buoyant spirits.

It was a fair wind now, and with a long day in front, and the freshness of Monday after a good rest. Still this was a rather more anxious day than the others, because in those though we had passed over the dangers on the coast of the Somme, they were hidden by water; and on a sunny morning who can realize shoals that are so fatal in bad weather, but are concealed by the smiling calm of a fine day? Not so with the great beetling cliffs of sharp red flint now glittering alongside my course for miles and miles far beyond what the eye could reach. These formed an impressive object ever in sight, and generally begetting, as it was seen, an earnest hope that the weather might be good "just to-day." This part of the coast, too, besides being iron-bound, has no port that is easy to enter, and the tides, moreover, are very powerful, so that, with either a gale or a calm, there would be a danger to meet.

It is obvious, of course, to the sailor who reads this that the difficulty of navigation along such a coast was much increased by my being alone. An ordinary vessel would put well out to sea, and go on night and day in deep water with a good offing, and its crew would take watch and watch until they neared the land again close to their destination.

But the course of the *Rob Roy* had to be within seven or eight miles of the shore, so as to keep within reach of a port at night, or at the worst near some shallower spot for anchorage; else, in the attempt to sleep, I might have been drifted twenty miles by the tide, perhaps out to sea, right away from our course, and perhaps ashore on the rocks. It had not yet become my plan to pass whole nights at sea as was necessary in the latter part of this voyage.

With these little drawbacks now and then, which threw rather a graver tone into the soliloquy of the lonely traveller, it was still a time of excessive enjoyment. The noble rocks towered up high on the left, and the endless water opened out wide on the right with only some dot of a sail, hull down, far far off on the horizon, a little lonely speck fixed in hard exile; but very probably the crew in that vessel, too, were happy in the breezy morn, and felt themselves and their craft to be the very "hub of the universe."

In a nook of the cliffs was Etretat, now the most fashionable bathing-place of Northern France. Long pointed pillars of rock stood in the sea along this shore, one especially notable, and called the "Needle of Etretat." Others were like gates and windows, with the light shining through. I thought of looking in here to escape the flood-tide which was against me, but I was deterred by the Pilot-book telling in plain words, "The Eastern part of the beach at Etretat is bordered by rocks which uncover at low water."

The *Rob Roy*'s previous behaviour in a sea made me quite at ease about waves or deep water, but to strike on a rock would be a miserable delay, and somehow I became more cautious as to exposing my little craft to danger the more experience I acquired; certainly also she was valued more and more each day. This increase together of experience and of admiration, begetting boldness and caution by turns, went on until it settled down into a strange compromise—extreme care in certain circumstances, and undue boldness at other times.

78

All over the British Channel there are patches of sand, shingle, or rock, which being deep down are not dangerous as regards any risk of striking upon them, but still even without any wind they cause the tide-stream to rush over them in great eddies, and confused babbling waves. The water below is in action, just like a waterfall tumbling over a hill, and the whirlings and seethings above look threatening enough until you become thoroughly aware of the exact state of the case, being precisely that which occurs above Schaffhausen, on the deeps of the Rhine, and which we have described in the account of a canoe voyage there.

These places are called by the French *ridèns*, or in England "ridges," and in some charts, "ripples" or "overfalls," and while there is sure to be a short choppy sea upon them, even in calm weather, the effect of a gale is to make them boil and foam ferociously.

A somewhat similar feature is the result when a low bank projects under water from a cape round which the tide is rushing; and as I determined not to risk going into Etretat, we had to face the tedious tossing about off one of these banks, described thus in the Pilot-book:—

"Abreast Etretat the shoal bottom, with less than eight fathoms on it, projects a mile to the N.N.W. from the shore, and when the flood-stream is at its greatest strength it occasions a great eddy, named by the mariners of the coast the *Hardières*, which extends to the northward as far as the Vaudieu Rock, and makes the sea hollow and heavy when the wind is fresh from the eastward."

It was just because the wind was fresh from the eastward that I could hope to stem the tide and get through this place; but once in the middle of the hubbub, the wind went down almost to nothing, so that for three or four hours I could only hold my place at most, and the wearisome monotony here of "up and down" on every wave, with a jerk of all my bones each time, was one of the few dull and disagreeable things of the whole voyage.

A sea that is "hollow" is abominable. However high a wave is, it may still have a rounded and respectable shape, and it will then tilt you about smoothly; but a "hollow" sea splashes and smacks and twists and screws, and the tiring effects on the body, thus hit right and left with sudden blows, is quite beyond what would be anticipated from so trifling a cause.

At length, as the tide yielded, the wind carried me beyond the Hardières, on and on to Fécamp, where the *Rob Roy* meant to stop for the night. But, willing though I was to rest there, the appearance of Fécamp from the offing was by no means satisfactory. It did not look easy to get into, and how was I to get out of it to-morrow? The Pilot-book took a similar view of this matter.*

Yet we must put in somewhere, and this was the nearest port to the Cape Antifer, the only remaining point to be anxious about, and which we might now expect to round next day. On the other hand, there was the argument, "If the wind chops round to the west, we may be detained in Fécamp for a week, whereas now it

* "Fécamp Harbour is difficult to enter at all times, and dangerous to attempt when it blows hard from the westward on account of the heavy sea at the entrance; for should a vessel at that time miss the harbour and ground upon the rocks off Fagnet Point, she would be totally lost."

is favourable; and if we can possibly get round to-day—— Well what a load of anxiety would be done with if we could do that!" The thought, quite new, seemed charming, and, yet undecided, I thought it best to cook dinner at once and put the question to the vote at dessert.

It is very puzzling what name to give to each successive meal in a day when the first one has been eaten at 2 a.m. If this is to be considered as *breakfast,* then the next, say at nine o'clock, ought to be luncheon, which seems absurd, though the Americans call any supplemental feeding a "lunch," even up to eleven o'clock at night, and you may see in New York signboards announcing "Lunch at 9 p.m. Clam Chowder."*

Now, as I had often to begin work by first frying at one or two o'clock in the moonlight, and as it would have a greedy sound if the next attack on eatables were to be called "second breakfast," the only true way of settling this point was to consider the first meal to be in fact a late supper of yesterday, or at any rate to regard it as belonging to the day bygone, and therefore beyond inquiry, and so to ignore this first breakfast altogether in one's arrangements. The stomach quite approved of this decision, and was always ready for the usual breakfast at six or seven o'clock, whatever had been discussed a few hours before.

The matter as to Etretat was decided then. We two were to go on, and to hope the wind would do so too. Then away sped we merrily singing, with the new and unexpected prospect of possibly reaching Havre that very day. From thence a month was to be passed in going up and down the Seine and at Paris; and what

* A mysterious shell-fish delicacy.

was to come after that? How come back to England? Why that must now be "blinked," as a future if not an insoluble question, at any rate just as easy to solve a month hence as it is now.

For a long time the wind was favourable, and precisely as strong as was desirable, and the formidable looking Cape Antifer, which at midday seemed only a dark-blue stripe on the distant horizon, gradually neared us till we could see the foam eddying round its weather-wasted base. Then came the steep high wall of flint cliff with shingle débris at its foot, but no one approach from top to bottom, if any bad thing happened—no, not for miles.

This was a time of alternate hope and fear, as the wind gradually lulled away to nothing, and fog arose in the hot sun; the waves were tossing the *Rob Roy* up and down, and flapping the sails in an angry petulant way, very distressing if you are sleepy. For four hours this hapless state of things continued, yet we were already within five miles of Cape de la Hève, and, once round that, on the other side was Havre. How tantalizing to be so near, and yet still out of reach! If this calm ends in a west wind, we may be driven back anywhere by that and the tide. If it ends in a thunderstorm we shall have to put off to sea at once.

See there the lighthouses up aloft on the crag—two of them are lighted. Soon it will be dark around, and we shall at this rate have to enter Havre by night. All this time we were close to the cliffs, but the sounding-lead showed plenty of water, and when the anchor was thrown out the cable did not pull at all; we were not drifting, but only rocked by the incessant tumble and dash of the sea, which, though of all things glorious when careering in the breeze, is of all most tiresome when rolling in a calm.

At this time I felt lonely, exceedingly lonely and helpless, also sleepy, feverish, discontented, and miserable. The lonely feeling came only twice more in the voyage; the other bad feelings never again.

Now, there are one or two sensations which after experience at sea seldom deceive you as to what they prognosticate, though it is impossible to give reasons for their hold upon the mind. One is the feeling, "I am drifting," another, "The water is shoaling," and the third, "Here comes a breeze." Each of these may be felt and recognized even with your eyes shut. It does not come in through one sense or another, but it seems to grasp the whole system; and it is a very great convenience to have this faculty alive in these three directions, and to know when to trust it as a true impression.

On the unmistakable sensation that a breeze was coming, the rebound from inaction and grumbling, lying full-length on deck, to alert excitement was instantaneous and most pleasing. The anchor was rattled up in a minute, and it was scarcely stowed away before the genial air arrived, with ripples curling under its soft breath, once more exactly favourable.

Slowly the two lights above on the cliff seemed to wheel round as we doubled the Cape. Slowly two little dots in the distance swelled up into big vessels in full sail, and others rose from the far-off waters, all converging to the same port with myself; their very presence being companionship, and their community of purpose begetting a mutual interest. For these craft deep in the water the navigation here is rather intricate,

though the excellent and uniform system of buoys employed in France does all that is possible to make the
course clear; but my little boat, drawing less than three
feet of water, could run safely even over the shallows,
though, as a rule, I navigated her by the regular
channels, as this gave me much additional interest in
the bearings about every port.

When the lights at Havre hove in sight the welcome
flashing was a happy reward to a long day's toil, and as
the yawl sped forward cheerily through the intervening
gloom, the kettle hummed over the lamp, and a bumper
of hot grog was served out to the crew. Soon we
rounded into the harbour, quiet and calm, with everybody asleep at that late hour; and it was some time
more before the *Rob Roy* could settle into a comfortable
berth, and her sails were all made up, and bed unrolled,
and the weary sailor was snoring in his blanket.

Next day the people on the quays were much amused
by the curious manœuvres of my little dingey; its
minute size, its novel form (generally pronounced to be
like a half walnut-shell), its bright colour, and the
extraordinary gyrations and whirlings which it could
perform, for practice taught some new feat in it almost
every day.

At night there was a strange sound, shrill and loud,
which lasted for hours, and marred the calm eve and
the quiet twinkling of the stars. This came from a
hundred children collected by a crack-brained stranger
(said to be English). These he gave cakes and toys to
by day lavishly, and assembled them at night on the
quay to sing chorus to his incoherent verses—a proceeding quite wonderful to be permitted by the police so
strict in France.

CHAPTER VI

The Seine—A wetting—Pump—Locks—Long reach—Rouen—
Steering—Henpecked—British flag—The captain's wife.

HAVRE was a good resting-place to receive and send
letters, read up the newspapers, get a long walk, and a
hot bath, and fresh water and provisions. Bacon I
found, after many trials to cook it, was a delusion, so I
gave mine to a steamboat in exchange for bread. Hung
beef, too, was discovered to be a snare—it took far too
long to cook, and was tough after all; so I presented a
magnificent lump to a bargee, whose time was less precious and his teeth more sharp. Then one mast had to
come down in preparation for the bridges on the Seine;
and therefore with these things to do, and working with
tools and pen, all the hours were busily employed until,
at noon on June 26, I hooked on to a steamer, *Porteur*,
with its stern paddles, very common in France, to be
towed up the river; a long and troublesome voyage of
about 300 miles, so winding is the course to Paris by the
Seine.

This mode of progress was then new to me, and I had
made but imperfect preparations, so that when we
rounded the pier to the west, and met the short, snappish sea in the bay, every wave dashed over me, and in
ten minutes I was wet to the skin, while a great deal of
water entered the fore-compartment of the yawl
through the hole for the chain-cable at that time left
open.* The surprising suddenness of this drenching

* Thick paper round my parcels of books within happily kept
them dry.

was so absurd that one could only laugh at it, nor was there time to don my waterproof suit—the sou'wester from Norway ten years ago, the oilskin coat (better than macintosh) from Denmark last year, and the canvas trousers.

A good wetting can be calmly borne if it is dashed in by a heavy sea in honest sailing, or is poured down upon you from a black cloud above; but here it was in a mere river-mouth, and on a sunny day, and there was no opportunity to change for several hours, until we stopped at a village to discharge cargo. The river at that place was narrow, and all the swell I thought was past; so, after a complete change of clothes, it was too bad to find in a mile or two the same story over again, and another wetting was the result. The evening rest was far from comfortable with my bedding all moist, and both suits of clothes wet through. One has therefore to beware of the accompaniments of being towed. The boat has no time to go over the waves, and, long rope or short, middle or side, steering ever so well, the water shipped when a heavy boat is swiftly towed must be as well prepared for as if it were in a regular gale on open sea.

The *Rob Roy* had now in the hold a great deal of water, and for the first time I had to apply the pump, which, having been carefully fitted, acted well. An india-rubber tube leading down to the keel was in such a position that I could immediately screw on a copper barrel and work the piston with one hand, so as to clear the stern compartment. By turning a screw-valve I could let the water come from the centre compartment, if any was there, and then I went to the fore-compartment, about seven feet long, which held the spare stores,

86

and a curiosity in the shape of a regulation chimney-pot hat to be worn on state occasions, but which was brought out once a week merely to brush off the green mould.

At noon the steamer set off again, dragging the yawl astern, and soon entered the first lock on the Seine, where the buildings around us, the neat stone barriers, and the dress and the very looks of the men forcibly re-called to my mind the numerous river locks passed in my canoe trips, but in so different a manner, by running the boat round every one of them on the gravel or over the grass.

The waste of time now in passing through each lock was prodigious. While nearing it the steamer sounded her shrill whistle to give warning, but still the lock was sure to be full of barges and boats. Then our cavalcade had to draw aside until the sluggish barges in front had all come out, and we went into the great basin with bumps, and knocks, and jars, and shouting. It required active use of the boat-hook for me to get the *Rob Roy* into the proper place in the lock, and then to keep her there. The men were not clumsy nor careless, but still the polished mahogany yawl had no chance with the heavy floats and barges in a squeezing and scratching match, and it was always sure to go to the wall.

Time seemed no object to these people, they were no doubt paid by the day. The sun shone upon them, and it was pleasant simply to exist and to loiter in life, so why make haste? Finally, we ascended as the lock filled, and then a second and a third joint cut off from our too long tail of barges had to be passed in also. After all, the captain and sometimes the whole crew deliberately adjourned to the lock-keeper's house for a

Long reach

"glass" and a chat; and when that was entirely done, and every topic of the day discussed, they all came back and had another supplemental parliament on the steamer's deck, like ladies saying "good-bye" at a morning visit; so that, perhaps, in an hour from beginning it, the work of ten minutes was accomplished, and the engine turned again once more—a tedious progress. Thus it was that four nights and part of five days were passed in mounting the Seine.

The scenery on the banks is in many places interesting, in a few it is pretty, and it is never positively dull. The traffic on the river is considerable above Rouen; but as there are two railways besides, few passengers go by water. The architecture and engineering on this fine river are indeed splendid. The noble bridges, the vast locks, barrages, quays, barriers, and embankments are far superior to ours on the Thames, though that river floats more wealth in a day than the Seine does in a month.

The sailors and dockmen were eager for my cargo of books; and among the various odd ways by which these had to be given to men on large vessels, there is one where the cabin-boy of a steamer looking through the round deadlight with an imploring request in his face, stretched out an eager hand to catch the book lifted up on the end of one of my sculls.

Then the neatness and apparent cleanliness of the villages, and the well-clothed, well-mannered people—also so "respectable." France is progressing by great leaps and bounds, at least in what arrests the eye. Its progress in government, liberty, and politics, is perhaps rather like that in a waltz.

Life in a towed yacht, alone on the Seine, is a somewhat hard life. You have to be alert, and to steer for sometimes twenty hours a day, and to cook and eat while steering. At about three o'clock in the morning the steamer's crew seemed suddenly to rise from the deck by magic, and stumble over coal-sacks, and thus abruptly to begin the day. We stopped about nine o'clock at night, and the crew flopped down on deck again, asleep in a moment, but not I for an hour or two.

As the grey dawn uncovered a new and cloudless sky, the fierce bubblings in the boiler became strong enough to turn the engine, and our rope was slipped from the bank. Savoury odours from the steamer soon after announced to me their breakfast cooking, and the *Rob Roy*'s lamp, too, was speedily in full blast. Eggs or butter or milk were instantly purveyed, if within reach at a lock; sometimes delicious strawberries and other fruits or dainties, the only difficulty was to cook at all properly while steering and being towed.

It is easy to cook and to steer at sea without looking up for many minutes. The compass tells you by a glance, and if not, the tiller has a nudge which speaks to the man who knows the meaning of its various pressures, through any part of his body it may happen to touch. But if you forget to steer constantly and minutely in a heavy boat towed on a river, she swerves in an instant, and shoots out right and left, and dives into banks or trees, or into the steamer's side-swell, and the man at the wheel turns round with a courteous French scowl, for he feels by *his* tiller in a moment, and you cannot escape his rebuke.

There was no romance in this manner of progress up the river. The poetry of wandering where you will, and all alone, cannot be thrown around a boat pulled by the nose while you are sitting in her all day. The *Rob Roy*, with mast down, and tied by a tow-rope, was like an eagle limping with clipped pinion and a chained foot. Still, for the man not churlish, there is scarcely any time or place or person wholly devoid of interest, if he is determined to find it there.

.   .   .   .   .   .

For the night we stopped usually in towns, but once or twice we rested in a great bend of the river where the steamer was run straight into the trees and made fast ashore exactly as if it were on the Mississippi and not on the Seine.

That thousands of solitary fishermen should sit lonesome on the river was the same puzzle to me as it had been before in canoeing on other French streams. Their silence and patience, during hours of this self-inflicted isolation, were incredible for Frenchmen, fond as we at first think all of them to be of *billard*, café, or dancing puppies, of anything, in fact, provided it assumes to be lively.

One thing I am at last decided about, that it is not to catch fish these men sit there; and the only reasonable explanation I can find of the phenomenon is that all these meek and lone fishermen are husbands unhappy at home!

There are numerous sailing-boats and rowing-boats on the Seine; but I did not see one that there was any difficulty in not coveting—their standard of marine beauty is not ours. All rigs and all sizes were there, even to a great centre-board cutter, twenty-five feet broad, and any number of yards long, in which the happy yachtsman could sail up and down between two bridges which bounded him on either side to a two miles' reach!

The French national flag is perhaps the prettiest on the world's waters; but as it is repeated to the eye by every boat and building, the sight of it becomes tiresome, and suggests that absence of private influence and enterprise so striking to an Englishman in every French work. Then again their sailors (not to say their landsmen) in very many instances do not even know our English flag when they see it, our Union Jack or ensign flying free on every shore.

At first I used to carry the French flag as well as our British jack out of compliment to their country, but as I found out that even in some of their newspapers the *Rob Roy* was mentioned as a "beautiful little French yacht," I determined that *that* mistake at any rate should not be fostered by me, so down came the tricolor, and my Cambridge Boat Club flag took its place.

In one reach of the river we came upon a very

unusual sight for a weekday, a French yacht sailing. Her flag was half-mast high, and she was drifting down the stream a helpless wreck. A distracted sort of man was on board, and a lady, or womankind at least, with dishevelled locks (carefully disordered though), the picture of wan weary wretchedness, and both of these hapless ones entreated our captain to tow their little yacht home. But, after a knowing glance, he quickly passed them in silence, and another steamer behind us also rounded off so as to give the unhappy pair the widest possible berth. Perhaps both captains preferred English sovereigns to French francs.

I was charged about £3 for being towed to Paris; but the various steamers (six in all) I employed on the river were every one well managed, and with civil people on board. Indeed, I became a favourite with one captain's wife, a sturdy-looking body, always cutting up leaves of lettuce. She gave me a basin of warm soup, and I presented her with some good Yorkshire bacon. Next day she cooked some of this for me with beans, and I returned the present by a packet of London tea, a book, a picture of Napoleon, and another of "the *Rob Roy* on the Seine," in the highest style of art attainable by a man steering all the time he is at the easel.

From all this it will be readily understood by anyone who has travelled much in various ways, that to be towed up the Seine is quite different from all other modes of progress, and that it brings you among a large, new, and sharply defined class of people, who could scarcely be known, and certainly could not be studied so well in any other way.

Nor is the traveller less interesting to these people than they are to him. Often it was necessary to restrain the inquisitive French *gamins*, who would teaze a boat to pieces if not looked after; but it is always against the grain with me to be strict with boys, especially about boats, for I hold that it is a good sign of them when they relish nautical curiosities.

CHAPTER VII

Dull reading—Chain boat—Kedging—St. Cloud—Training—
Dogs—Wrong colours—My policeman—Yankee notion—Red,
White, and Blue.

THE effect of living on board a little boat for a month at
a time with not more than three or four nights of usual
repose, was to bring the mind and body into a curious
condition of subdued life, a sort of contemplative
oriental placid state in which both cares and pleasures
ceased to be acute, and the flight of time seemed gliding
and even, and not marked by the distinct epochs which
define our civilized life. Although this passive enjoyment was really agreeable—and, in fine weather and
good health, perhaps a mollusc could affirm as much
of its existence,—certainly an experience of the condition I have described enables one to understand what
is evidently the normal state of many thousands of hard-
worked, ill-fed, and irregularly sleeped labourers; the
men who, sitting down thus weary at night, we expect
to read some prosy book full of desperately good advice,
of which one half of the words are not needed for the
sense and the other half are not understood by the
reader.*

The last tug-boat we had to use was of a peculiar

* Very few authors can write books suitable for men with weary
bodies and sleepy minds. It is remarkable to see how much
attention these men will pay to the words of the Bible and the
"Pilgrim's Progress." No doubt such readers often read but the
surface-sense of both these books; but then even that sense is good,
and the deeper meaning is better, while the language of both is
superb.

kind, and I am not aware that it is employed upon any of our rivers in Britain. A chain is laid along the bottom of the Seine for (I think) two hundred miles. At certain hours of the day a long solidly built vessel with a powerful engine on board comes over this, and the chain is seized and put round a wheel on board. By turning this wheel one way or the other it is evident that the chain will be wound up and let down behind, while it cannot slip along the river's bottom—the enormous friction is enough to prevent that, and therefore the boat is wound up and goes through the water. The power of this chain-boat is so great that it will pull along, and that too against the rapid stream, a whole string of barges, several of them of 300 tons' burthen. The long fleet advances steadily though slowly, and the irresistible engine works with smokeless funnels, but there are groanings within, telling of tight-strained iron, and loud undertoned breathings of confined steam.

Although the chain-boat is not often steered for the purpose of avoiding other vessels (they must take care of their own safety), yet it has to be carefully managed by a rudder, one at each end, so that it may drop the chain in a proper part of the river for the next steamer of the Company which is to use it. When two such boats meet from opposite directions, and both are pulling at the same chain, there is much time lost in effecting a passage, and again when the chain-boat and all its string of heavy craft arrives at a lock, you may make up your mind for a long delay. It is evident that we do not require this particular sort of tug-boat on the Thames below Teddington, for the strong tide up and down twice every day carries along thousands of tons of merchandise at a rapid pace, and one or two men will be enough to attend upon each barge. In fact, we have the sun and moon for our tugs. These draw the water up, and the tide is the rope which hauls our ships along.

To manœuvre properly with the *Rob Roy* in such a case as this with the chain-boat required every vigilance, and strong exercise of muscular force, as well as caution and prompt decision, for I had sometimes to cling to the middle barge, then to drop back to the last, and always to keep off from the river-banks, the shoals, and the trees. On one occasion we had to shift her position by "kedging" for nearly half a mile, and this in a crowded part of the Seine too, where the current also was swift. On another occasion the sharp iron of a screw steamer's frame ran right against my bow, and at once cut a clean hole quite through the mahogany. Instantly I seized a lump of soft putty, and leaning over the side I squeezed it into the hole, and then "clinched" it (so to speak) on the inside; and this stop-gap actually served for three weeks, until a proper repair could be made.

The lovely precincts of St. Cloud came in sight at dawn on the last day of June, prettier than Richmond, I must confess, or almost any river-town we can boast of in England; and here I was to rest while my little yawl was thoroughly cleaned, brightly varnished, and its inside gaily painted with Cambridge blue, so as to appear at the French Exhibition in its very best suit, and then at the British Regatta on the Seine.

Some days were occupied in this general overhaul, during which the excellent landlady of the hotel where I slept must have been more amazed even than she declared, to see her guest return each day clad in blue flannel, and spattered all over with varnish and paint, for the captain was painter as well as cook. Of course all this was exchanged for proper attire after working hours.

In the cool of the morning, three fine young fellows are running towards us over the bridge; lithe and easy step, speed without haste. White flannel and white shoes. They have come to contend at the regatta here, the first of an invasion of British oarsmen, who soon fill the lodgings, cover the river, and waken up the footpath early with their rattling run. Some of these are brown-faced watermen from Thames and Humber and Tyne, others are ruddy-cheeked Etonians or University men, or hard-trained Londoners, and others have come over the Atlantic; John Bull's younger brothers from New Brunswick, not his cousins from New York. You might pick out among these the finest specimens of our species, so far as pluck and muscle make the man.

Few of the French oarsmen could be classed with any of the divisions given above. Rowing has not attained the position in France which it holds in England. For much of our excellence in athletics and field sports we have to thank our much-abused English climate, which always encourages and generally necessitates some sort of exercise when we are out of doors.

But it is a new and healthy sight on the Seine, these fine fellows running in the mornings, and it gives zest to our walk by the beautiful river.

Here also as we stroll about, two dogs gave much amusement to us: one was a Newfoundland, who dashed into the water grandly to fetch the stick thrown in by his master. The other was a bulldog, who went in about a yard or so at the same time, and then as the swimmer brought the stick to shore the intruder fastened on it, and always managed somehow to wrest the prize from the real winner, and then carried it to his master with the cool impudence which may be seen not seldom when the honour and reward gained by one person are claimed and even secured by another.*

From the truck to the keel the *Rob Roy* had been thoroughly refreshed and beautified. The perfection of a yacht's beauty is that nothing should be there for only beauty's sake. It is in the observation of this strict rule that the English certainly do excel every other nation; and whether you take a huge steam-engine, a yacht, or a four-in-hand drag, it is almost generally allowed, and is certainly acknowledged by the best connoisseurs of each, that ornament will not make a bad article good, while it is likely to make a good one look bad. Even the flags of a yacht have each a meaning, and are not mere colours. Therefore they ought to be made, at all events, perfectly correct first, and then as pretty and neat as you please. I examined the flags of all the boats and yachts and steamers at the Exhibition; and there was wonderfully little taste in their display, nearly every one—English and foreign—was cut wrong, or coloured wrong, or too large for the boat that carried them. Even our Admiralty Barge, where specimens of boats from England were exhibited, had a flag flying, with the

* Many phases of human character may be studied among dogs. If men's vices are matched by dogs' failings, several of our best virtues are at least equalled by those in canine characters; courage, fidelity, and patience especially. One might well devote a whole hour in London to observe the dogs in the streets,—to look at dog-life solely, and forget all besides. It is hard to believe (even if indeed we are at all warranted in believing) that these noble animals are done with existence when they die. It is harder still to see a man cruel to a dog, without feeling pretty sure that the man is not the better of the two.

stripes in the jack quite wrong. She was the only craft on that side of the Pont de Jena; but as it was the English side (though some English yachts had gone to the other side), I anchored there, right opposite the sloping sward of the Exhibition, and I did this without asking any questions. It is best now and then to do right things at once, and not to delay until time is wasted in proving them to be right.

To write after a visit to the Exhibition and *not* to describe it, will be a double good—to him who writes and to those who read of his visit. Of the Paris hotels and lodgings, too, I have no traits to give, because I did not use them, but slept on board my little craft in perfect comfort, and could spend all the rest of the day on shore. Each morning about seven o'clock you might notice a smart-looking French policeman standing on the grass bank of the Exhibition, and staring hard at the *Rob Roy*. He had come to see her captain at his somewhat airy toilette, and he was particularly interested, if not amazed, to witness the evolutions of a toothbrush. Perhaps he found them not only interesting but instructive, and involving an idea perfectly new—hard also to comprehend from so distant an inspection. Surely this strange implement must be a novelty imported from England for exhibition here.

As he gazed in wonder at the rapid exercise, I sometimes gave the curious instrument an extra flourish above or below, and the intelligent and courteous gendarme never rightly decided whether or not the toothbrush was an essential though inscrutable part of the yacht's sailing gear. Our acquaintance, however, improved, and he kindly took charge of the boat in my absence; not without a mysterious air as he recounted its travels (and a good deal more), to the numerous visitors,—many of whom, after his explanations, left the *Rob Roy* quite delighted that they had seen "the little ship which had sailed from America!"

The boat *Red, White, and Blue* he thus confounded

My policeman

with mine was at that time not far off, in a house by itself, amid the other wonders which crowded the gardens of the Exhibition. The two venturesome Americans who came to Europe in this ship had but scant pleasure either in their voyage itself or in their visit to France and England. Storm, wet, and hunger on the wide Atlantic were patiently borne in hopes of meeting a warm welcome in Old England; but, instead, they had the cold chill of doubt. Much of their sufferings in both these ways were directly due to their own and their friends' mismanagement, the stupid construction of their cabin, the foolish three-masted rig of their boat, the boastful wager of the boat's builder, and their imprudence in painting up the boat on her arrival, and tarring the ropes; and, lastly, in allowing a mutilated paper to be issued as their "original log."

Disappointed here, they turned to Paris, expecting better days. Fair promises were made. Steamers were to tow the boat up the Seine in triumph; but it was towed against a bridge and smashed its masts. Agents were to secure goodly numbers to visit her; but for three months scarcely anyone paid for a ticket, until at length the vessel was admitted into the grounds of the Exhibition. Finally, the ruined Captain ran away to England, but cleverly contrived to carry his ship with him. Whatever may be thought as to the wisdom or advantage of making such a voyage and in such a boat, it is a very great pity that when it has been effected there should be a failure in appreciating its marvellous accomplishment.

The possibility of taking a boat across the Atlantic, with west wind prevailing and with no rocks or shoals to fear, is altogether beyond doubt. The ill-fate of two other boats that have tried the feat shows how dangerous it is to try. But after examining, probably more than anybody else, the evidence in their case —the men, the log, the documents, and affidavits, and the boat, and its contents, also the numerous doubts and criticisms from all quarters, both in London and Paris, and in Dover and Margate, I have good reason to believe that the "Red, White, and Blue" had no extraneous help in her voyage across that wide ocean. The unexplained wonder is that men able and willing to perform such a deed as this should be incapable of building and rigging their boat so as to do it comfortably.

·   ·   ·   ·   ·   ·

CHAPTER VIII

THE *Rob Roy* was very pleasant lodgings when moved down to the lovely bend at St. Cloud. Sometimes she was made fast to a tree, and the birds sung in my rigging, and gossamers spun webs on the masts, and leaves fell on the deck. At other times we struck the anchor into soft green grass, and left the boat for the day, until at night returning from where the merry rowers dined so well in training, and after a pleasant and cool walk "home" by the river-side, there was the little yawl all safe on a glassy pool, and her deck shining spangled with dewdrops under the moon, and the cabin snug within—airy but no draughts, cool without chill, and brightly lighted up in a moment, yet all so undisturbed, without dust or din, and without any bill to pay.

Awake with the earliest sun, there was always the same sound alongside as we lay at anchor. The sweet murmurings of the water running by, cleft by my sharp bow, and gliding in wavelets along the smooth sides only a few inches from my ear, and sounding with articulate distinctness through the tight mahogany skin; and then there was the muttering chatter of the amateur fisherman, who was sure to be at his post, however early.

This respectable personage, not young but still

103

hearty, is in his own boat,—a boat perfectly respectable too, and well found in all particulars, flat, brown, broad, utterly useless for anything but this its duty every morning.

Quietly his anchor is dropped, and he then fixes a pole into the bottom of the river, and lashes the boat to that, and to that it will be fixed until nine o'clock; at present it is five. He puts on a grey coat, and brown hat, and blue spectacles, all the colours of man and boat being philosophically arranged, and as part of a complicated and secret plot upon the liberties of that unseen, mysterious, and much-considered *goujon* which is poetically imagined to be below. It has baffled all designs for this last week, for it is a wily monster, but *this* morning it is most certainly to be snared.

Rod, line, float, hook, bait, are all prepared for the conflict, and the fisherman now seats himself steadily in a sort of arm-chair, and with stealth and gravity drops the deceitful line into hidden deeps. At that float he will stare till he cannot see. He looks contented; at any rate, no muscle moves in his face, though envy may be corroding his soul. After an hour he *may* just yield so much as to mutter some few sounds, or a suppressed moaning over his hard lot (and that is what I hear in my cabin). Then at last he rises with a determined briskness in his mien, and the resentment against fate from an ill-used man, and he casts exactly three handfuls of corn or bread-crumbs into the water, these to beguile the reluctant obstinate gudgeon, who, perhaps, poor thing, is not so much to blame for inattention after all, being at the time just one hundred and fifty yards away, beside those bulrushes.

Indeed, that very idea seems to have struck the

fisherman too, and he marks the likely spot, and will go there tomorrow, not today—no, he will always stick one day at one place. How he moves to or from it I do not know, for the man and boat had always come before I saw them, and I never stopped long enough to see them depart. Four men fished four mornings thus, and only two fish were caught by them in my presence.

The regatta is over, and Nadar's balloon is in the sky, but seeming no bigger than other balloons, so soon does the mind fail to appreciate positive size when the object you look at is seen alone. It is the old story of the moon, which "looks as large as a soup-plate," and yet Nadar's *Géant* is the largest balloon ever seen, and it carries a house below it instead of a car,—a veritable house, with two storeys, and doors and windows. The freedom of its motion sailing away reminds me that the *Rob Roy* ought to be moving too—that she was not built to dabble about on rivers, but to charge the crested wave; and, indeed, there was always a sensation of being pent up when she was merely floating near the inland cornfields, and so far from the salt green sea; and this, too, even though pleasant parties of ladies were on board, and boys got jaunts and cruises from me, which I am certain pleased them much: still the reef-points on her sails rattled impatiently for real breezes and the curl of the surf, while the storm mizen was growing musty, so long stowed away unused.

Next day, therefore, the Blue Peter was flying at the fore, and the *Rob Roy*'s cellar had its sea stock laid in from "Spiers and Pond," of ale, and brandy, and wine. Before a fine fresh wind, with rain pelting cheerfully on my back, we scudded down the Seine. To sail thus along a rapid stream with many barges to meet, and trees overhanging, and shoals at various depths below, is a very capital exercise, especially if you feel your honour at stake about getting aground, however harmless that would be. But the Seine has greater difficulties here, because the numerous bridges each will present an obstacle which must be dealt with at once, and yet each particular bridge will have its special features and difficulties, not perhaps recognized when first you meet them so suddenly.* The bridges on the Seine were often not high enough to allow the yawl to pass under, except in the centre, or within a few feet on one side or other of the keystone, and as the wind is deflected by the bridge, just at the critical moment when you reach such places, and the current of water below rushes about in eddies from the piers, there is quite enough of excitement to keep a captain pretty well awake in beating to windward through these bridges; for the wind *must* be dead ahead a great part of the time, because the river bends about and about with more and sharper turns than almost any other of the kind.

Though sun and wind had varnished my face to the proper regulation hue, in perfect keeping with a mahogany boat, yet the fortnight of fresh water had softened that hardiness of system acquired in real sea. My hands had gradually discarded, one after another, the islands of sticking-plaster, and a whole geography of bumps and bruises, which once had looked as if no

---

* I recollect that old Westminster Bridge was a very dangerous one for a boat to sail through, because the joints between the *voussoirs*, or lines of stones under the arch, were not horizontal as in most other bridges, but in an oblique direction, and several times when my mast has touched one of these it was borne downwards with all the power of a screw.

gloves ever could get on again—or rather as if the hands must always be encased in gloves to be anywhere admissible in a white-skinned country.

But now once again outward bound, though still so many miles from the iodine scent of the open sea, and the gracious odour of real ship's tar, one's nerves are strung tight in a moment. The change was hailed with joy, though sudden enough, from the glassy pond-like water at St. Cloud, lulled only by gentle catspaws, half-asleep and dreaming, to the rattling of spars and blocks, and hissing of the water, in the merry whistling gale by which we now were rapt away.

At Argenteuil there are numerous French pleasure-boats, and the *Rob Roy* ran into a good berth. Next day there was a downright gale, so I actually had to reef before starting, because in a narrow river the work of beating against the wind is very severe on legs and arms, and especially on one's hands, unless they are hardened, and kept hard, too, by constant handling of the strong ropes.

At length we put into a quiet bay, where the River Oise joined the Seine, and we moored snugly under the lee of a green meadow, while trees were above waving and rustling in the breeze. It was far from houses, for I wished to have a good rest, as the tossing of the former night had almost banished sleep.

But soon the inquisitive natives found the yawl in her hiding-place, and they sat on the grass gazing by the hour. The surroundings were so much like a canoe voyage, that I felt more strongly than ever the confinement to a river, while the sea would have been so open and grand under such a breeze. Therefore I gave up all idea of sailing down the Seine any more, and decided to get towed to Havre, and to launch out fairly on our proper element once more.

Yet it was fine fun to row about in the dingey, and to discover a quaint old inn, and to haul ashore my tiny cockle-shell and dine. Here they were certainly an uncouth set, they did not even put a cloth on the table, nor any substitute for it—a state of things seen very seldom indeed in the very outermost corners of my various trips.

Faithful promise was made by a man that he would rouse me from slumber in my cabin under the hay-bank at the passing of the next steamer, be it light or dark at the time. The shriek of the whistle came in the first hours of morning, and the man ran to tell it, with one side of his face shaven, and the other frothed over with lather.

Being towed down is so like being towed up the river, that we need merely allude to a few features in the voyage westward.

At one pretty town we stopped to unload cargo for some hours, and I climbed the hills, scaled the old castle walls, and dived into curious tumbledown streets. The keeper of the newspaper-shop confessed to me his own peculiar grievance, namely, that he often sent money to England in reply to quack advertisements, but never had any reply. He seemed to be too *poli* to credit my assertion that there are "many rogues in perfidious Albion," and on the whole he was scarcely shaken in the determination to persevere in filling their pockets, though he might empty his own.

An old man at a lock was delighted by a New Testament given to him. "I know what this is: it is Protestant prayers. Oh, they are good." Then he brought his wife and his grandchildren, and every one of them shook hands.

It was not very easy to get one's sea-stores replenished in the continuous run down the Seine. Sometimes I saw a milkman trundling his wheelbarrow over a bridge, and, jumping on shore, I waylaid him for the precious luxury, or sent off a boy for bread, and butter, and eggs; but, of course, the times of eating had nothing to do with any hours, or recurring seasons for a meal: you must cook when you can, and snatch a morsel here or there, in a lock or a long reach of the stream. At night the full moon sailed on high, and the crew lay down with their faces over the steamer's side, chatting with their English comrade till it was far past bed-time, for we shall be off at three to-morrow morning.

The steam in the boiler first warns of the coming bustle as its great bubbles burst inside, and rattle the iron plates. Then, being more frequent and tighter bound, they give out a low moaning, hidden rumble; and if the boat touches the side of the steamer, there is a strong vibration through all her sonorous planks, until some tap is turned in the engine, and the rush of steam leaps into the cylinder as if indignant at its long restraint. You had better get up now (there is no dressing, for the simple reason that there has been no undressing), and in two minutes you are fresh and hearty, though it is only a few hours since you dropped to rest.

Rouen looks as if it would be all that is pleasant for a sailing-boat to rest in. Never was a greater deception. It is difficult to find an anchorage, and impossible to get a quiet berth by the quay. The bustle all day, and the noise all night, keep you ever on the tenterhooks;

though, as these discomforts are caused by the active commerce of the port, one ought to bear them patiently.

In one of the numerous *mêlées* of barges, boats, and steamers whirling round and round, amid entangled hawsers, and a swift stream, we had at last to invoke aid from shore, and a number of willing loungers gladly hauled on my rope. Some of these men, when I thanked them, said they had more to thank me for—the books I had given them in my voyage up. Still, with all this aid, the *Rob Roy* was inextricably entangled with other heavier craft, and, in shoving her off, I tumbled overboard, and had to put up with a thorough wetting; so, after a warm bath ashore, more *à la mode*, I returned to my little cabin for a profound sleep.

Rain, almost ceaseless for a whole day and night, had searched the smallest chink, and trickled ungraciously into my very bedroom. But I suspended an iron teacup in the dark just over my body, so that one little stream was intercepted. This was the first really hard pressure of wet on the *Rob Roy*, and all the defects it brought to light were entirely remedied afterwards at Cowes.

On each of the four preceding nights I had been aroused for the next day's work at three, or two, or even one o'clock, in the dark, and yet for one night more there was to be no regular repose.

My mast had been made fast to the quay wall, but in forgetfulness that on a tidal river this fastening must be such as to allow for several feet of fall as the water ebbs. Therefore, about the inevitable hour of one o'clock, in the dark, there was a loud and ominous crack and jerk from the rope, and I knew too well the cause. In the rainy night it was a troublesome business to arrange matters, and next day was a drowsy one with me, spent in the strange old streets of the town.

The policeman had orders to call me at any hour when a steamer went by, and, being hooked at last to the powerful twin-screw *Du Tremblay*, with a pleasant captain, I rejoiced to near the very last bridge on the river, with the feeling at heart, "After this we are done with fresh-water sailing."

It was a suspension-bridge, and the worthy captain forgot all about the *Rob Roy* and her mast, when he steered for a low part, where his own funnel could pass because it was lowered, but where I saw in a moment my mast must strike.

There was no time to call out, nor would it have availed even to chop the towing-line with my axe, for the boat had too much "way" on her to stop. Therefore I could only duck down into the well, to avoid the falling spar and the splinters.

The bridge struck the mast about two feet from the top, and, instead of its breaking off with a short snap, the mast bent back and back at least four feet, just as if it were a fishing-rod, to my great amazement. The strong vibration of its truck (*pomme* the French call it), throbbed every nerve of boat and man, as it scraped over each plank above, and then the mast sprang up free from the bridge with such a switch, that it burst the lashings of both the iron shrouds merely by this rebound.

Now was felt the congratulation that we had carefully secured a first-rate mast for the *Rob Roy*, one of the pieces of Vancouver wood, proved, by the competitions lately held, to be the strongest of all timber.

The moments of expected disaster and of happy

relief were vivid as they passed, but I made the steamer stop, and on climbing the mast, I found not even the slightest crack or injury there. Henceforth we shall trust the goodly spar in any gale, with the confidence only to be had by a crucial test like this.

As we shall soon be at sea again, but the river is calm enough here, perhaps this will be a fit opportunity for the reader to peep into *Rob Roy*'s cave, as it was usually made up for the night.

The floor of the cabin is made of thin mahogany boards, resting on cross-beams. The boards are loose, so that even in bed I can pull one up, and thus get at my cellar or at the iron pigs of ballast. The bed is of cork, about seven feet long and three feet wide. On this (for it *was* rather hardish) I put a plaid,* and then a railway rug, which being coloured, had been substituted for a blanket, as the white wool of the latter insisted on coming off, and gave an untidy look to my thick blue boating-jacket.

One fold of the rug was enough for an ample covering, and I never once was cold in the cabin. A large pillow was encased by day in blue (the uniform colour of all my decorations), and it was stripped at night to be soft and smooth for the cheek of the sleeper.

Putting under this my coats and a regulation woven Jersey, with the yacht's name worked in red across its breast in regular sailor's fashion, the pillow became a most comfortable cushion, and the woodcut shows me reclining in the best position for reading or writing,

---

* I found that a common Scotch plaid, if it was in an inclined position, resisted wet longer than any other material permeable to air, and it could be readily dried by hanging it from the mast in the wind.

as if on a good sofa. On my right hand behind is a
candle-lamp, with a very heavy stand. It rests upon a
shelf, which can be put in any convenient place by a
simple arrangement.

In the sketch already given at p. 58, there is a tar-

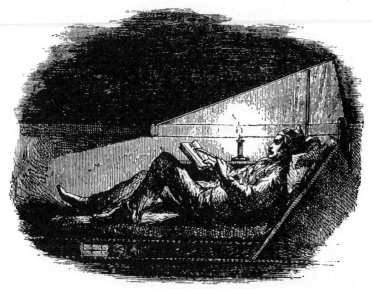

The cabin

paulin spread over the well, and this was used on one
occasion when we had to cook in rain while at anchor.*

* There was another method of cooking under shelter, and we
employed it on the only other occasion when this had to be done,
namely, to shut up the cabin and to cook inside it, using the port-
able "canoe cuisine". But as this is meant to be employed only
on shore, it does not answer well on board, except in a calm; and,
moreover, the heat generated by the lamp was too much in a little
cabin. Even a single candle heats a small apartment, and it is well
known that a man can get a very good vapour-bath by sitting over
a rushlight, with blankets fastened all round.

On the same side, and below the boxes, "Tools" and "Eating," already mentioned, are two large iron cases, labelled "Prog"—a brief announcement which vastly troubled the brains of several French visitors, whose English etymology did not extend to such curt terms.

In these heavy boxes are cases of preserved meats, soups, and vegetables, and these I found perfectly satisfactory in every respect, when procured at a proper place (Morel's in Piccadilly). Here you can get little tin cases, holding half a pint each and sealed up hermetically.*

To cook one of these tins full—which, with bread and wine is an ample dinner—you cut the top circle with the lever-knife, but allowing it to be still attached by a small part to the tin, and fold this lid part back for a handle.

Then put the tin into a can of such a shape and size that it has about half an inch of water all round the tin, but not reaching too high up, else it may bubble over when boiling, and as you can use salt water or muddy water for this water-jacket, it will not do to sprinkle any of that inside the tin.

The can is then hung over the Russian lamp, and in six minutes the contents of the tin are quite hot. Soup takes less time, and steak perhaps a little more, depending on the facility of circulation of the materials in the tin and the amount of wind moderating the heat. The

* The best, according to my taste, were those of "Irish stew," "Stewed steak," "Mulligatawny," "Ox-tail," and "Vegetable soup," all in the order named. "Preserved peas" were not quite so good; but the other viands were all far better than can be had at any ordinary hotel, and were entirely without that metallic or other "preserved" flavour so soon discovered in such eatables, and even by a palate not fastidious.

preserved meat or soup has been thoroughly cooked before it is sold, and it has sauce, gravy, and vegetables, and the oxtail has joints, all properly mixed. Therefore, in this speedy manner your dinner is prepared, and indeed it will be smoking hot and ready before you can get the table laid, and the "things" set out from the pantry.

Concentrated soup I took also, but it has a tame flavour, so it was put by for a famine time, which never came. As for "Liebig's Extract of Meat," you need not starve while there is any left, but that is the most we can say in its favour.

CHAPTER IX

High tide—Seine pilot—To bed—Terrible scene—A tumble in—
In the swell—Novel steering—Puzzled—Night thoughts—The
Start—A draft on the deck—Balloon jib—On the deep.

On the Seine there is a tide phenomenon, called the *barre*, as in English rivers the *bore*, which, when not provided for, is very dangerous, especially at spring tides. The water then rushes up the narrowing funnel-shaped estuary, in a broad and swelling wave, sometimes four feet high, and this will sweep off even large vessels from their anchors, and it causes many wrecks.

On a former occasion, when I happened to be in this neighbourhood, a high tide had been truly predicted by astronomers, which would culminate at the little town of Caudebec on the Seine, but would also rise higher than ever known before on all the adjacent coasts.

The news of this coming wonder spread over France, and there being then a lull in Europe as to revolutions, &c. (except, of course, the perennial revolution in Spain), the *quidnuncs* of the provinces had to run to the coast for an excitement. Excursion trains, and heavily laden steamers poured volumes of people into Caudebec, and many of them had never seen salt sea before. At the fashionable bathing-town of Trouville the sight was a strange one when thousands of expectant observers paraded the soft white sand as the full moon shone on a waveless sea, and the brilliant dresses of the ladies coloured the beautiful tableau.

The tide flowed and flowed; it bubbled over the usual bounds of the shore; it trickled into the bathing-

116

sheds; it swelled still higher upon the trim-kept prome-
nade, until it lapped the highest point and then went
gently down again. Eclipses and tides are patent proofs
to the people that physical science can appeal to. The
"music of the spheres" hath also a true rhythm, "There
is neither speech nor language but their voices are
heard."

To escape this *barre* on the Seine, our steamer
anchored by the quaint old town of Quillebœuf with
other vessels; and, though the wind howled and the rain
poured, the hill beside us sheltered all from its blasts,
which were too wild and powerful in the sea outside to
allow us to proceed next day.*

However, our Seine pilot pointed to an English
steamer "which dared not go out"; so any remonstrance on the subject was silenced, and then he boldly
asked if I would like a pilot on board the *Rob Roy*
(towed by the steamer all the time), and I had sufficient
command of countenance to decline with due gravity.
Better, perhaps, it would have been for me not to carry
then so much of the John Bull into these strange waters,
as will be seen from what occurred that night.

The tide rushed up with extraordinary strength, until
it was quite full. Then it paused for five minutes, and
again it set off in the opposite direction with the same
fury, increased, too, by the stream and the wind being
also down the river.

At each of these changes every vessel, of course,
swung round to its anchor, and so must have loosened its

* Frenchmen have a trick of anchoring thus to escape a breeze.
We have seen them anchor on the African coast merely to avoid a
hard-looking cloud, whereas the real danger was in anchoring
there at all.

hold, while all the water picture changed from right to left like a scene shifted on the stage. During this short interval of quiet you could row ashore, but to get back again was almost impossible when the full torrent of water ran in straight.

As night came on I noticed that our steamer's anchor was dragging, and that other steam vessels, more on the alert, were easing the strain on their cables by working their engines at half-power all the time.

"Captain, we are dragging anchor." "No, sir," he said, "you are mistaken." "I am sure we are dragging: I have watched for ten minutes." "No, sir, I am certain we do not drag." He said this with such firmness, that I confidingly believed it, and turned into bed.

But it was not to sleep, except in fitful snatches. The sound of the water hurrying by my side, like a mill race, and within a few inches of my ear, had a strange and unwonted effect, not now to soothe, but to drive sleep away. Bits of wood and other *débris* often struck my mahogany sounding-board with a loud thump, until I became accustomed even to this, and was in a dreamy dozing about one o'clock.

Then there came a new noise—a low, steady rap, tap, tap, tap on the boat, and from underneath. For a moment or two there was sensation without apprehension—a sort of mesmeric, irresistible spell; but a sudden thought burst through the trance, and with a powerful impression of what was doing—one no less horrid than true—I dashed off covering, roof, hatchway, and all, and stood upon deck to meet a terrible scene.

Our steamer had drifted in the dark until we closed upon another steamboat astern. My yawl, tied to the stern of one, was between that and the bows of the

It was successful, and I fell into the water

other, the anchor chain of which had already got underneath the waist of the *Rob Roy*, and had been ringing the rap, tap, tap of a warning that undoubtedly saved her life. Light flashed from the riding lamp at the steamer's bow full on my boat's deck, which was now heeled over deeply until the dark water rushed through her gunwale; it seemed that only a few seconds more and the poor little yawl would sink in the flood, or be ground into splinters by the two great iron monsters nearing each instant in the dark.

All this was noticed in the same rapid glance which in such dangers grasps a whole scene in a moment and stamps it in the mind for years.

My boat hung on the cold iron chain, yet it wavered with equal poise to go this way or that. If she could be swerved to the stern she might possibly escape destruction, but if to the other side, then the strong rope at her bow would entirely prevent her escape. With a loud shout to arouse the crews I put every atom of bodily force into one strenuous shove, straining nerve and muscle in the desperate effort until I could not see. She trembled and surged—it was successful, and I fell into the water, but my yawl was saved.

Crash came the two steamers together. I heeded nothing of their din and smashing, and the uproar of the men, but I had scrambled all wet into my cabin, nervously shaking with excitement and a chattering of teeth. Then I sat down to sum up my bruises—a barked shin, sprained thigh, and bleeding cheek-bone; and a hapless object I must have seemed, bathing by turns, my leg, and shin, and face, from a brandy bottle, and then a gulp inside. In a survey of the yawl made next day, there was to be seen (as still there is) the mark of the iron chain-links deeply impressed in the mahogany planks of her waist. The piece of wood that bears these mementoes of that night's deed might well be cut out and kept as a curious memorial. The bowsprit also was found to have been nipped at the end (though it had been drawn in close to the stem), and the squeeze had quite flattened the strong iron ring upon it, and jammed up the wood into a pulp as if it were cork.

The weather did not moderate next day, but we started nevertheless, and when the waves of the wider sea were tumbling in I expected to have a wetting, as in passing here before; but the sea was in fine long swells, and so the yawl rode over them buoyantly. Also the large twin-screw tugboat is far more pleasant to follow than the smaller steamer with its two paddle-wheels, one at each side of the stern.*

In another way also I managed better than before while undergoing the process of being towed. I set the hatch of the well in front of me, and then allowed the reflection of the funnel of the steamer upon the wet deck of my boat to be seen through a chink, while my head and body were entirely concealed and completely sheltered from spray.

Now, having marked where this reflection rested, when I was exactly in a proper line abaft the steamer, I was enabled to steer altogether by the shadowy image, although I could not see the object itself to which I was

* This latter construction is found to be very convenient, because the cargo is at one end of the vessel and the machinery, and paddle-wheels, and steering apparatus are all at the other end, so that orders can be readily given to both by the captain. The "Express" Company on the Seine has sixty of these steamers.

directing the bow of my boat. The captain and crew of the steamer were very much astonished with this proceeding.*

Arriving at Havre on July 21, there was need for a good rest, and the port was well suited for it. There is quiet water in a sequestered nook of the harbour and plenty of amusement on shore. Havre, too, was in a state of much excitement, for the Empress was about to embark thence for England, and the Imperial yacht was in the basin, with a splendid crew on board. In the evening the Emperor also came to the town, to escort his wife when she embarked, and as his carriage drove past the crowd ran after it hallooing.

The beautiful English yacht *Vindex* was on the gridiron with the *Rob Roy*; that is to say, on a sunk stage of wood, on which you can place a vessel, if it is desired to examine or repair its hull and keel when the tide leaves it there dry.

Vindex had come to the Havre Regatta, and as she had won the prize there in the previous year a great deal of interest was shown about her now. But the regatta on this occasion was by no means interesting, for the wind fell into calm, and it was merely a drifting match.

* It was, however, only an adaptation of the same principle I had used in Swedish lakes, when my course was towards a bright sun so dazzling in the water that I invented the plan of covering my eyes with my straw hat, and steering the canoe by the bright reflection of the sun on its cedar deck, which was of course by no means so unpleasant as the beams of light glancing from the water itself. Surely it would not be impossible to make the needle of a mariner's compass itself steer the ship at least within half a point. The motion of the needle could connect one or the other of two electro currents, and so set in instant motion a powerful purchase to act on the tiller.

My usual visits in the dingey had disposed of nearly all my store of French books and periodicals, and the remainder we took to a civil bookseller, from whom we bought French charts and a Pilot-book of the English south-coast soundings.

Meantime, after a rest and refreshment to my crew, a thorough scraping to my boat, and a good stock laid in of comfort for my voyage to England, the question had to be distinctly put, "How am I to get over the broad Channel to the Isle of Wight?" It was, of course, impossible to think of coming back as we had gone—that is, along the French coast. This would never do. Again, it was also found that the steamers were not allowed to tow any boat to sea behind the passenger vessels unless in case of distress, so that put an end to another solution of the problem, which was to get half-way by towing and then to cast off and sail.

Well, shall I get an additional hand on board? But where is he to sit if it blows hard? And if it does not blow hard, what is the use of him? In fact, I was steadily driven, as if by severe logic, to the conclusion already at the bottom of my mind, to *sail right across alone.*

Then I asked one or two experienced sailors if they thought the *Rob Roy* could do it, and they said, "Yes, she can; but can *you*? You may be three or four days out, and can you stand the fatigue? At any rate, do not start in a south-west wind: it raises a sea, and the up and down of the waves will tire you soon in a long day's work, and then there is the night besides."

Having retired to my calm little creek, where the yawl was tied by a line to a large fishing-smack, I tried to read, but very soon found I was thinking of anything but the words on the printed page; then to sleep; but still I was musing on the prospect now opened of a hazardous and delightful sail.

About one o'clock I gazed out moodily on the quiet night scene of the harbour, sleeping around. Tall masts whitened by the moon, black hulls darkened in the shade, busy quays silent, long-necked iron cranes peering into the deep water that reflected quaint leaning houses, all distorted, and big buoys magnified by the haze.

"Why continue this anxiety about how to get over? See the clouds drift over the clear moon with an east wind. Will it ever be easier than now? I cannot sleep— why not start this moment?"

Once the decision was made, all was alert on the *Rob Roy*; and in half an hour I had breakfasted, and then very noiselessly loosed the thin line that bound us to the quay, and bid "adieu to France."

Every single thing we could think of was perfectly prepared. The sails were all ready to set, but we had to row the yawl slowly into the main harbour, and there we met a low round swell coming in from the sea. We tugged hard to force her against the adverse tide, but progress was tediously slow. Presently some fishing-luggers were getting under way, and soon the usual clatter and din of the French sailors, at full tide, rang forth as if by a magic call at two in the morning.

After shouting some time for a boat to tow me to the pier-head, at last one came.

"What will you charge?"

"Ten francs."

"I'll give you eight"; and after parley the two men in their little boat agreed to take the *Rob Roy* in tow.

Almost immediately I noticed that the moon was hid, and the wind had chopped round to the south-west, the very wind I was told not to start with, but now—well it was too late to withdraw, and so we laboured on, while the great clumsy luggers crossed and recrossed our course, and frequently dashed upon the piles of the pier in the stupidest manner, with much loud roaring of voices, and creaking of spars, and fluttering of sails.

Presently the men called out that, as the sea was getting higher, I had better pay them the money. "Certainly," I said; but, alas! could find only five francs of change, the rest being napoleons.

They shouted, "Give us gold—we will send the change to England"; but I bellowed out a better plan, to give them an order on the yacht agents at Havre for five francs, and the silver besides.

Finally this was accepted, so I got out paper and envelope, and on the wet deck, by moonlight, wrote the banker's draft.

When they came near the harbour's mouth, they sung out, "Get ready your mizen."

"Ay, ay!"

"Hoist"; and so up went the trim little sail, glad to flap once more in salt air. Then they bid me, "Get ready your jib—we have cast you off; hoist!" Yes, and I did hoist.

Perhaps the reader may recollect that the end of my bowsprit had been squeezed by a collision, and was in fact as weak as a charred stick. But I had entirely forgotten this, by some unaccountable fatality, during the three days at Havre, when it might have been easily repaired.

The moment therefore I had hoisted the jib, the

bowsprit end broke sharp off into a ragged stump, and the jib instantly flew away into the air, just like an umbrella blown inside out.

This was, of course, a most critical time for such a mishap, with a strong breeze dead ahead, driving me in upon piles, and a tumbling sea, and numerous large luggers sailing about me in the dark. Therefore I felt that this unlucky accident and the south-west wind meant, "I must not go out to-night. It will not do to begin a voyage of a hundred miles with a broken bowsprit."

All this prudent reasoning was at once cut short by the Frenchmen calling out, "*Voulez-vous sortir encore, monsieur?*" and the *Rob Roy* thus hailed could make but one reply, "*Oui, oui, certainement*"; so I bid them lay hold again while I captured the truant jib, hauled down and reefed it, and made it fast to the stem, and then again "*Lachez tous*," and we are free on the rolling waves.

At the worst, methought, we can return in four or five hours, when the tide falls, if we find it unadvisable to go on; but meanwhile our yawl shot away westwards, to get a good offing from the Cape de la Hève, and then I cooked breakfast (the former one counted, of course, in the former day, according to the excellent rule already explained), and about half-past four I laid on my straight course to old England, with a capital breeze on my quarter, and a hundred times glad that I had not gone back.

CHAPTER X

Nodding—Prancing—First thoughts.

Up rose the sun, and all was cheerful. Then I laid her to, and got out my axe, and chopped the bowsprit into shape, so that it would run out further, and then set the whole jib firmly on it.

All the feelings restrained so long by the river work, and regatta amenities, and Exhibition in Paris, now came forth powerfully in a flow of enthusiasm.

Boys seem to like the story of the canoe voyage, and perhaps they will read this one of the yawl. If they have a sailor turn, they will imagine the new pleasure to be felt when you glide away from a fast-retreating land, and nothing is in front but sea, sea, sea. Then the little boat you are in, and know in every plank, and love too, becomes more than ever cherished as a friend. It is your only visible trust, and, if it *is* a good boat, you trust it well, for indeed it seems to try its very best, like a horse on the desert plain, that knows it must go on if it is ever to get to the other side. Then as the cliffs, that looked high behind you, dwindle into a line of deep blue, the compass by your knees becomes a magic thing, with no tongue indeed to speak, but surely a brain it must have to know the way so well.

For hours we went on thus in silent pleasure, gazing at the gentle needle as it moved without noise; and, with nothing around but plash of waves, bright sun, and a feeling of hot silence, the spell of sleep was overpowering. Homer sometimes nodded, it is said, and he would have certainly had a good nap had he steered long thus. The sinking off into these delicious slumbers was imperceptible, and perfectly beyond the will's control. In a moment of trance I would be far away in dreamland, and with a thousand incidents, all enacted in orderly succession, with fights, wrecks, or pageantry, or the confused picture of bright-coloured nothings which fancy paints on the half-alive brain.

From these sweet dreams there was a rude awakening; a slap from the sea on my face, as the yawl, untended, suddenly rounded to, or a rattling taptoo on the deck when the jib-sheets found they were free.

Then for a time I would resolutely insist upon attention—every moment of slumber being a positive wandering from the course; but no, the outer self that demands a nap will not be denied by the inner nobler self that commands alertness.

Only one single sea-gull did I see in thirty hours. One vessel also, far off, was the sole break upon the painfully straight horizon, and as the wind gradually died away into nothing, the prospect did not improve.

Then came the up and down, riding over seas without gaining a yard, the "prancing" of the vessel which had galloped forth in the morning like a horse in its first bounds on grass when, leaving a hard road, its hoof paws gladly the springy turf.

Some feelings that came up then from deep recesses in the mind were new, but too new and unnamed to put in words. Alone on the waters, when you cannot see land, is a strange condition. However, if only fog or darkness hides the land, you still feel that land is there. Quite another thing is it to be afloat alone, where, because it is fifty miles away, land cannot be seen. Doubtless it may seem foolish, but I am not able to tell the feelings of that time.

. . . .

CHAPTER XI

SEE the sails are impatiently flapping. Each wave jerks the mast and canvas with a smart loud crack like that of a whip. The sound is unspeakably irritating, it seems so useless and wanton, and so perfectly *de trop* while the wind is absolutely calm. At other times, in such a case, you can stop this provoking clatter by hauling up the boom and lowering the jib; but here, in mid ocean, we must not hamper the sails but be ready for the first faint breath of wind, and moreover—best to confess it—I had in this case a serious disturbance *within*, yet not mental. Strawberries and cream imprisoned with mushrooms did not agree.

They called them mushrooms in Havre yesterday, and we know "there are 371 edible fungi"; but I assert that the rebellious species embarked with me were toadstools, and so giddiness followed upon sleep. . . .

Gentle and cool is the first fresh murmur of a new breeze as it comes from afar, tripping along. Gratefully we watch its footsteps on the sea. Its garments rustle in the south, and the glassy rounded waves are now crested by its touch. Then the coolness of it fans the cheek, the flag flutters while the sails fill full, the mast bows under the soft pressure, and the *Rob Roy* runs eagerly again upon her proper course.

Dinner was instantly served up to celebrate the event. It is an Englishman's way. Still we were fifty miles from England, but wave after wave rose, dashed, and was left behind, till the sun got weary in his march, and hung, in the west, a great red globe. My course had been taken for the Nab light, which is in the entrance towards Portsmouth, but the Channel tide, crossing my path twice, could carry the yawl fast, yet secretly, first right, then left, and both ways once again.

Yet when the evening shade fell we expected to see at least some light in the horizon, for the English lights are clear, and they shine out twenty miles to sea. How I peered into the inscrutable darkness, and standing by the mast to get higher, but in vain; yet still the wind urged on, and the sea tumbled forward all in the right way.

Hours passed, and ship-lights now could be descried; they were crossing my path, for they were in the great fair-way of nations bound east or west through the Channel. This at least was company, but it was also danger. We have left the lonely plain, and are walking now in the street of waters; but how am I to sleep here, and yet I *must* sleep this night. I tried to "speak" a goodly vessel sailing past like a shadow—I ventured even to near it—hailing, "How far to the Nab?" but the voice melted in the breeze. Low vapoury clouds began to rise from the sea; they looked like dark trees around; but the stars were clear up above. It was impossible not to feel as if land was there, yet, when my lead was cast, the deep only laughed at its little reach downward.

In such thick weather it will never do to ferret out the channel to Cowes, even if we are near it. The night must be passed at sea, and better begin to do that now than go in too near the cliffs in darkness, and so we prepared to lie-to. Lowering the main-sail, I tried the yawl first under mizen and jib; but the rolling in every trough of the waves was most uncomfortable, and besides she drifted north, which might end by going ashore.

Then I took in the jib and set the storm-mizen, and hung out the anchor with twenty fathoms of chain—not, of course, to reach the bottom, but to keep the boat's head easier in the sea, and this did perfectly well. The motion was a long, regular rise and fall, and the drift was to the east; quite out of our proper course, indeed, but I couldn't help that.

The motion of a vessel lying-to is far more easy than what would be supposed possible. When you are rocked in a boat, making progress by sails or steam, the pressure of each wave is more or less of a blow, for the ship is going forward, and it resists the mass of water often with violence. At anchor, too, though in a modified degree, the same is the action, and in a swell without wind the oscillations are jerky and short, for they are not softened by the sails then merely hanging. But if a boat is staunch and strong, and the deck is tight, and she has plenty of keel, so as not to swerve round right and left, but to preserve a general average direction towards the wind, then she may lie-to in a very stiff gale and high sea with a wonderfully gentle motion. Her head then is slightly off the sea, and there is but little rolling. The sails are so set that they ease every lateral heave. She forges forward just a little between the wave tops, and when the crest of one lifts her up she courteously yields for the time, but will soon again recover lost ground by this well-managed "compromise."

When we saw how admirably the *Rob Roy* behaved in lying-to, and that scarcely a wave broke over her deck, we felt that if it came to the worst we might thus pass a whole week in her safely.

Now I must make my bed. Undoubtedly this was a risky deed about to be done; but pray what else could we do?

"You ought not to have come there at all," may be replied.

Say that to the huntsman who has got into a field with the only way out of it over a chasm to leap. Tell it to the mountain climber scrambling down, who pauses before a *crevasse*; and do not forget to say the same to the poor old fisherman, overtaken in the midnight winter's gale, with his life in one hand and in the other a tangled net that has caught the fried sole for your comfortable dinner.

It would not do, of course, to go into my cabin. In the first place, the dingey was there, and then if I were to be enclosed inside when anything like a "run down" had to be dealt with, the cabin might be my coffin.

First I tried to crouch down in the well, but the constraint on limbs and joints was unbearable. My head slept while my knees ached with the pressure. No! there must be a positive lying down to sleep, if the sleep is to give true refreshment when you are rocked about on the waters; and this you have no doubt been convinced of any time at sea.

The strange twists of body I tried to fit into comfortably where the space was only three feet each way, reached at last to the grotesque—the absurd contortions of a man miserable on a pleasure jaunt—and I laughed aloud, but somehow it sounded hollow and uncanny.

As to the exact spot where the *Rob Roy* was at this particular time we had, of course, no possible idea, but judging from after circumstances, the position must have been about ten miles south of St. Catherine's Head, and she drifted twenty miles east while I dreamed.

One effect of extreme exhaustion is to make the mind almost reckless of risk, and we can well understand how in some shipwrecks, after days and nights without sleep, men are in a placid, callous composure of sheer weariness, and that the last agony of drowning then is nothing, just as Dr. Livingstone tells us, the shake given by a lion to his victim paralyses the whole system before it is killed. Therefore, as danger was only likely, and sleep was imperative, I must have sleep at all hazards, and so loosed out the folds of the main-sail on the wet deck. How white and creamy they looked while all was dark around, for no moon had risen. Then I put on my life-belt, and fastened the ship's light where it would not swing, but rested quite close to the deck. I rolled the thick, dry, and ample main-sail round me, stretching my limbs in charming freedom, and I tied myself to the boom, so as not to be easily jerked overboard by the waves. Of course it was my firm intention to sleep only by winks of one eye at a time; but the struggle with Morpheus was, we suspect, *very* faint; at any rate no record remained but a few dim visions that may have flickered in the soft vanishing of consciousness.

Can any person be expected to describe his first feelings as he awakes in such a bed and finds it broad day? Bright and glorious sun, high up, how I stared at you! and then a glance to the side, and behold, there is land—England. Deliberately I rose and gave three hearty cheers—nobody there to hear, indeed, but myself—no matter, it did good to me to cheer, and to hear too. Breakfast was soon agoing. Ten hours' sleep had thoroughly refreshed me, mind and body; but I could not make out what part of the coast we had hit upon.

It was still about twelve miles distant, and as there were no cliffs in sight, it could not be the Isle of Wight. My chart told nothing; my French Pilot-book had woodcut pictures of all the coast, but nothing came of the search in these; and whether we had drifted east or west of the Isle of Wight we finally gave up as a question —we must go to the coast itself and see.

Therefore we steered due north, rapidly nearing the unknown land, and with a joyous morning, barometer high, wind south, and a coming fine day. Presently there loomed on the horizon one, and then another, and another, splendid ships of war. They steamed in line, and I tried to intercept them to put the query, "Where am I?" Baffled in this, the puzzle was, "Are they going to Portsmouth or Plymouth?" There were equally good reasons for either.

At length three towns could be seen, and the pictures of the French Pilot-book were closely examined, but several plates had each three towns which would fit the case before me, one as well as the other. Fortunately we chose the middle one of the three, because it had a little lighthouse. That on the left we afterwards found was Bognor, which has a reef of dangerous rocks on its shore.

A fisherman was in his boat, and I hailed him, "Boat ahoy! What is the name of that town?"

"Town, sir?"

"Yes; that village right ahead; what do you call it?"

"The village there, sir?"

"Yes; what is its name? It has a name, hasn't it?"

"Oh, yes, certainly, sir, it's got a name."

"Well, what *is* the name? I don't know where I am."
"Where have you come from, sir? from the Wight?"

And, after these Scottish answers to the questions of a Scotsman, at last I found my way into Littlehampton; and if ever you go to the Beach Hotel in want of a soft bed, after sleeping out of a bed for nearly a month, you will find it there.

This little place, between Bognor and Brighton, is a quiet bathing-town just in the delicate stage of existence, when it has been found out and admired, but not yet spoilt. One row of houses fronts the sea with a fine grassy plain between, and a clean white strand.

The Inn is of olden times, and apart near the water, with a landlady of the good old English type; and her son, the waiter, rampant about canoes, keeps an aviary under the porch and a capital swimming dog in the stable.

Lie on a sofa in the coffee-room detached, and read *The Times*—go into the drawing-room and play the piano, or sit under the garden trees and gaze on the fair blue sea, and hope fervently that, with a strong Tory government to protect our institutions, this hotel may be long kept hid from that merciless monster the "Company (Limited)." But already a railway runs here, and threatens its quiet. Even a steamer now and then from France screws its way into the very narrow channel, where the River Arun has wound down thus far from Arundel.*

* The *Rob Roy* hopes to sail thither next summer, up the Thames, and by the canal, and the River Wey and the Arun, and so to Southsea. [In 1868 MacGregor made this voyage, leaving Erith on June 10th, going south by the Wey River down the Arun to Littlehampton, and thence to Bognor on the 20th, Portsmouth on the 23rd, arriving on June 27th at London after breaking bowsprit.]

CHAPTER XII

Heavy sea—Isle of Wight—The commodore—A glance at gear—
Bow—Running gear—Sisterhooks—Horse—Tiller.

THE boy and his dog formed a small crowd on the little pier to see the *Rob Roy* start again with a fine breeze off shore, but freshening every minute until near Selsea Bill it blew half a gale. The navigation round this point is difficult at low water, as may be seen from the markings in the chart copied at p. 173, merely as a specimen of what a chart is for the sailor's eye.

At last it was necessary to reef main-sail and jib, the wind blew so hard and in gusts, and the adverse tide met me as it rushed out of Spithead with a heavy swell. Rain poured down slanting with the wind, and the rocks, uncovered at low water, looked very un-inviting to leeward.

The little dingey was towed astern, as we had not expected so much sea with a north wind, but for the first time we found how perfectly this diminutive boat was adapted for towing, and after this trial she was never again stowed in the cabin. The bluff bow above, and the keelless, round, smooth bottom below, enabled the dingey to top the sharpest wave, and I often forgot my steering while turning round to watch the little creature as she nimbly leaped over the tumbling billows. The weather got worse, therefore we changed for a storm-mizen, and so many seas broke heavily over the *Rob Roy*, that the water in the well washed about my ankles, and finally we were compelled to give in and lie-to for an hour or more, after manning the pump.

This wind, rain, and sea together were the worst we had met with, but the yawl seemed in high spirits, like her owner; though the waves in the tide-way were sometimes so short and sharp that it was impossible to rise and fall fast enough, and she often buried deeply. It was here that my chart was so wet that it melted before my eyes, even with all endeavours to preserve it, and therefore I bore up for Brading Harbour, in the Isle of Wight, and somehow managed to get round Bembridge reef all safe into the quiet lake beyond.

Here, and on British soil again, was an end to all expected anxieties of the summer's voyage. The rest to come were to be met, but not anticipated. There had been first the goal of Paris to be reached at a certain time for the Regatta there, and then there was the unknown voyage over the Channel, homeward bound; but henceforth no more dates or wide seas had to be thought of, and the rest of the vacation was free.

The shores and seas about the Isle of Wight looked more cheerful and lovely than ever, with a fair day next morning. Here we soon pass one of the new sea-batteries, a huge granite castle, reminding one of Bomarsund, but unfinished, and with scaffolds round that are worked or stopped, as Ministries go out or in, and as guns or iron plates are proved strongest in turn at Shoeburyness.

Portsmouth is in front, always with moving life on the waves. A squadron of ironclads presses heavy on the water at Spithead, and among them conspicuous is the five-masted *Minotaur*. White-winged yachts glide through the blue space between these and Ryde. Osborne basks in the sunshine, with the "sailor Prince's" pleasure-boat by the shore. If there be a gap or two in the horizon it is soon filled up by some rich laden merchantman, with sails swelling full in the light, and gay signal flags flowing out bright colours; and all the scene is woven together, as it were, by swift steamers flitting to and fro like shuttles strung with a thread of foam across a warp of blue.

But it is to that wooded point at Cowes we are steering, and the tall yellow masts clustered there show already what an assemblage the yawl will meet at the Royal Yacht Squadron Regatta.

There was a certain amount of sailor's pride as our yawl steadily advanced, steering in among these, the smallest of all, but ready to be matched against any of its size and crew. She quietly approached the crowded quay, and I put my portmanteau ashore at the Gloucester Hotel; then the jib was filled again to sail up straight to Medina dock, where Mr. John White would see the craft he had modelled, and after a careful survey, the verdict upon her was entirely favourable.*

On her safe arrival at Littlehampton, after crossing the Channel, a short account of the voyage had been sent to *The Times*, and this had reached the numerous yachtsmen at Cowes an hour before the boat herself appeared in front of the Club house. Therefore, the little craft required no more introduction. My flag was my card, and I was speedily made a member of the Club for the time being. Many old friends here greeted me, and many new visitors came on board to

---

* After so much experience of the yawl, tried in all points in all kinds of wind and weather, it may well be supposed that numerous improvements had been noted in my book as desirable. These, however, we need not here particularize, as the various descriptions given at intervals through this book show what the *Rob Roy* is in her latest and best arrangements.

congratulate, while His Royal Highness the Commodore of the Canoe Club, whose burgee flew at my mast-head, graciously shook hands.

While the ship carpenters at Medina dock are making my new bowsprit, and a hundred other things, and Mr. Ratsey is putting the last finish to my sails, we may examine a little the upper gear of the yawl, as that has not yet been specially noticed; but as ladies and landsmen often come on board, who do not require a minute description of all the ropes and spars in the *Rob Roy*, they can skip the rest of this chapter.

From the sketches of the yawl given in our pages, it will be seen at once that she was under-masted and under-sailed. She could bear a spread of canvas double of that she carried; but for safety, for handiness, and for comfort, we must be content to sacrifice some speed.

Therefore, it was only in a very powerful breeze that the beautiful build and lines of the hull had anything like fair play for showing her pace through the water. *Then*, indeed, and when others were reeling about and shipping seas, even under reefed canvas, the *Rob Roy* at once asserted her position.

We have spoken of the excellent mast already. The shrouds were of iron rope. This is affected by heat and wet, but not so much as cordage is. The screw links to tighten the shrouds seldom had to be employed; a copper rope from the truck to a shroud acted as a lightning conductor.

The bowsprit is on the starboard side, for this allows you to use the right hand with the chain-cable in the bitts. The jib has a foot of nine feet in stride. Its tack is on a rope round an open hook at the bowsprit end, so that in reefing you can get it in without danger of falling overboard, while reaching out to detach it; then it is hooked on the stem. An iron bobstay we discarded, and an iron forestay, as difficult to keep taut; but after trials with no bobstay at all, we found it advisable to replace this, although it is a troublesome rope in dealing with the anchor.

The gunwale has an opening of half an inch all round, and this was enough for scuppers.

The forehatch is thirteen inches square, so that I can readily squeeze down into the fore-cabin.

I painted about a foot of the chain-cable of a bright-red colour, at ten and at twenty fathoms, which was useful in telling how much ran out with the anchor. Fenders I got in Paris, very neatly made of line net-work, over canvas bags of cork.

The iron sheave on the stem for the anchor-chain was large, with a high cheek, and the comfort of this was well appreciated in weighing anchor at night or in a swell. The jib-sheets led aft, and the position of the cleats for these was most carefully chosen, as they are more worked than any part of the rigging; yet this position was twice altered, and the best place seems to be on the deck, two feet forward from your breast and two feet to the side.

The strain on these sheets in rough weather was greater than had been anticipated, and at last I had to put a tackle on the port jib-sheet, as that is the one less conveniently placed for belaying.

The peak halyard was fast to the gaff, then through a single block on the mast and one on the gaff, and again one aloft. The throat halyard was fast to the mast, and through a block on the throat, and then aloft. Both these halyards came down on the starboard side, and to separate cleats, but I found it generally more ready to haul on the two at once, and belay them together.

The jib-halyard had a block on the sail, and then, with the topping lift, came down on the port side. A jib purchase I soon cut away—one learns to be economical of action when alone. Each of these four ropes then passed through a sheave on deck, two on each side, in an iron frame, properly inclined to give a clear lead.*

Sisterhooks are troublesome things. Some much better plan as a substitute has to be invented, but I used for their mousings india-rubber rings, which answered perfectly well, and were easily replaced at six for a penny.

Stocking and re-stocking the anchor were the only operations when I felt the want of another hand, either to do the work at the bow or to give that one touch to the tiller at the critical moment, which an infant could do when near it, but which is hard for a man at a distance. The anchors were on deck, one at each side of the bitts, and fitting securely within the gunwale.

Two things, above all, I must try to devise for next voyage—a cleat that will need no bends, but hold anywhere instantly, and an anchor-stock, self-acting in dark, rain, and wind, and without a forelock to slip out or get jammed.

The hatch of the well was in two parts, and one of them, a foot in breadth, had chocks on each side, so that in rain and dashing spray it was fixed up at an

---

* The fall of each halyard was coiled and put under the taut part. A small coil looks neatest, but the fall of it is sure to kink if coiled close, being wet and dry ten times in a day. Before nearing harbour, or in preparation to lower sail "handsomely," I found it well to cast the coil loose on the hatch, else a kink would catch in the leading sheave.

angle before me, and thus only my eyes were above it exposed, and by moving my head down slightly I could see the compass and the chart. A tarpaulin of one-faced indiarubber over the sloping board and under the horse had its loose folds round one of my shoulders to the weather side, so that even in very rough water not much could get into the open well.

The main-boom had a ring working between cheeks, and carrying a double block with a single block below. To reduce the long fall of the sheet I altered the upper block to a single one; but in the first heavy weather afterwards it was found to be too small a purchase. The force of the wind is underrated if you reason about it in fair weather.

The sheet block was fast to a strong, plain, copper ring, as a traveller, and after much trouble and expense about a horse for this, trying first an iron one, then a copper rope, and then hemp, I found that a rounded inch bar of red iron-wood straight across and about two inches above the bulkhead of the well, answered to perfection.*

The oars were stowed one on each side of the hatch combing with blades aft, and looms chock up to the gunwale at the bows, so as to be seldom moved by a rush of sea along the deck, and yet one or other or both could be instantly put into the iron crutches always kept ready shipped, and so placed that I could row

---

* The bar presented a very smooth surface for the bottom of the dingey to run over when it was shipped under the hatch, or hauled out in a hurry. Moreover, the wood was convenient to stride across in getting from the well to the cabin, and it was far more pleasant and *warmer* than metal to hold on by during violent lurches of the sea.

comfortably while in the well and facing the bow. The boathook had its handle-end always near my right hand, and this saved me many a run forward in awkward times.

The tiller of iron-wood was well wedged into the rudder-head. Of course any joggling or slackness here is like a broken front tooth or a loose steel pen. No plan that I heard of, or saw, or could devise yet, is entirely satisfactory for enabling the tiller to be set fast in a moment, at any angle, and yet to be *perfectly* free in ordinary times. I used a large piece of rough cork as a wedge to set the tiller, and a cord loop at each side of the gunwale, to keep it "hard down" when going about. At night, to stop the vibration of the rudder, I knocked in a brass wedge between its head and the iron bushing of the rudder hole.

Every bit of iron above water was galvanized; but this operation weakens small pieces of iron unless it is carefully done. However, the only part which carried away was my small anchor-stock, and this took place at the first cast of it into the Thames.

Such is the *Rob Roy* yawl, of 4 tons register, and the map at p. 188 shows the general course of her first sea voyage by a dotted line, but many a long mile of zigzag had to be sailed besides.

CHAPTER XIII

MEDINA DOCK is the place to see all sorts of ships and
boats for steam, sailing, or rowing, lifeboats, rafts, and
models. The basin is full of broken-backed men-of-war,
whose old black bones are being disjointed and dragged
asunder here to make strong knees again, just because
they are black and well-seasoned. Alongside the quay
we had seen the three American yachts, which came
across the Atlantic amid many English cheers for
the vessels of two hundred tons crossing from New
York, while we scarcely record the voyages of our
own hundred-ton vessels that have often sailed to
Australia.

In Mr. White's garden there are Chinese junks and
catamarans afloat in a pond, and even the walls around
are not allowed to be quite of dry land, being painted
with sea soundings and charts of the neighbouring
coasts. This may indeed be called the Admiralty of the
yacht fleet, and Cowes is its Portsmouth.

"*Nauta nascitur non fit*," which is in English, "British
boys are ducklings born to the water."

Now many of these have affectionate parents not
web-footed, and the filial duty of a little duck to the
motherly hen is a very difficult question of conscience
when a pond is near; but then there is no positive need
to boat, while there *is* a positive command to obey.
This solves the question with all brave loving boys, who

K   145

are manly enough to obey the woman dearest on earth to them.

A little vessel two feet long may be called a toy ship, but it is a toy that can teach much to an Admiral, and I should not like to have as my comrade on a voyage the man of forty who can pass the Serpentine without a glance at the little ragged urchin there, who is half in the water himself while he reaches with a twig his tiny lugger after its long voyage across the lake among ducks, and row-boats, and billows two inches high.

Victoria Park, again, has a feast of nauticalities now and then for boys who love boats, when the Model Yacht Club sails its lilliputian squadron for a half-crown cup.

The competing yachts first lie on the green grass for inspection. They are made in "off hours" by working men, who sail as well as build them. Wife or a school-girl daughter has sewed the sails, and the paint on the hull is gorgeous. Crowds of all classes and ages are at the starting-post, and when the pistol fires the cheers begin. Each favourite in the fleet has its admirers, who run alongside, and the Secretary alone has a grave face, as of a man on important duty. Who can say what sailors' seedlings may be watered in that pond, and to grow up in manhood afterwards as hearts of oak?

And if a boy is too young, or lazy, or clumsy-fingered to make a boat for himself, let him go along Fleet Street till he comes to the spot where he can turn his back upon St. Dunstan's church. Depend upon it he will cross over to the *Model Dockyard* there, and after buttoning his jacket over his watch-chain, and a good shove down to his pocket-handkerchief, if he has one, let him

146

wriggle in by elbow and knees till he gets a good place among the crowd at the window.

Even when it is time to go home he will not have seen half the naval stores here, or the little sailors—from Cork—all waiting to be engaged; but if he buys the *Illustrated Handibook* inside from Mr. Lawrence, to con over at home, perhaps at his next visit he may be admitted upstairs to a delicious treat, where he can gloat over the more hidden fleet of the future.

Some, perhaps many, people keep yachts who do not enjoy sailing. We have sometimes seen a yacht-owner who could not steer his own dingey. There are others whose chief anxiety when once on board is for their speedy arrival at the next port. To have the best yacht of the year is no sign of its owner being a good sailor. The horse that wins the Derby would most likely not be first if he carried his owner, and a man may have a good carriage who cannot himself "handle the ribbons."

It is no discredit to anybody that he is not able to ride a race or steer a schooner, or drive a drag; but it is well to remember more than we do whose is the skill that wins in each of these exercises.

At Cowes one perceives very soon that a good deal of *yachtomania* is fed upon the good meat and drink afloat, and balls and promenades ashore, and the pomp and bustle of getting from one to the other, not to forget the brass buttons which fasten more vulgar minds to some Clubs. Leaving aside all these in peace, provided they play with the thing as they have a right to do, and as openly as now, so that none can mistake them, we have still left to be admired a splendid set of fellows, yes, and of women too, who really love the sea. We know a hardy canoeist who said he would not marry anybody unless she could "pull bow oar," and it must be a great addition to the family hearth when the help-meet can "mind her luff."

In the regatta week the tide of a congregation coming out of the pretty church at Cowes is thoroughly aquatic. Fine stalwart men with handsome faces, girls with chignons as big as a topsail bunt, yacht skippers of bronze hue and anxious eye, well-fed sailors with cerulean Jerseys, children with hat ribbons and neckties labelled with yacht names. There were 150 yachts on the water here and the *Rob Roy* anchored close to the Hotel, from which the sight was magnificent at night, when each mast-light was hung, and the whole made a brilliant crescent reflected in calm sea, while excellent music played softly on shore, and at each half-hour the bell of every vessel tolled the time, *Rob Roy* adding her note to the jingle by so many thumps with an iron pot.

Near the yawl was a strange little cutter of five tons, as remarkable for the number of people on board it as mine was for having so few. There was the grey-haired hearty papa, and when we had noticed him taking observations with a sextant, we knew he was "a character." Then there was his active son, and a younger brother, and a sister in bright red, and a sailor boy. They looked even more numerous, because they kept for ever moving out of sight, and then appearing in new costume, under and above the awning like a large umbrella spread on their boom.

It was a treat to lunch with this kind hale yachtsman, and to see the one minute cabin full of mirrors, pictures, statuettes, crockery, and furniture. To make room for the visitor two of the inhabitants ate their share of a huge pie in the punt alongside.

Then, to rise at once to the largest yacht of them all, there was the beautiful *Zara*, a schooner of 315 tons, fitted out for a Mediterranean cruise, but making her first voyage from Cowes to Southampton, convoyed by the *Rob Roy*, and as her reefing topsails and her Flemish horse got entangled aloft by new stiff ropes, she drifted against another fine schooner; but with cool heads and smart hands on board of each of them, the pretty craft were softly eased away from a too rough embrace, and no damage was done.

About twenty of the yachts were steamers, and at least as many besides had steam launches, a new adjunct rapidly becoming popular, and which soon will be almost a necessary for every yacht of 200 tons. All of these that I saw were lifeboats, built on "Lamb and White's" principle, that is, with air chambers along the sides, so that they decline to upset, and if they are filled by the sea, they are not only still floating but steady also.

The Royal National Lifeboat Institution build boats with ballast below and with air chambers so disposed at the ends and in the bottom as to cause the boat to right itself when it has been overturned, while Mr. S. White's boats are constructed so as rather to prevent a capsize than to right the boat afterwards.

During an experimental trial in a heavy sea, one of these side-chamber boats was intentionally overturned, and it then kept steadily floating bottom upwards, so that the crew clambered up safely on the keel, where the handles provided for the purpose enabled them to hold on. Of the fourteen men, however, only thirteen could be counted, and so it was found that "Jem" was missing; but when he was called, Jem answered from the *inside* of the boat, "All right!" "What! Are you inside?" "Yes, I'm looking for my cap." He was safe enough in the vacant space between the water and the floor, upturned over him, and there was room for several more of the crew inside.

The two rival systems then seem to represent (1) a boat which will speedily right, of which the men, if upset, may float outside until she rights, or keep inside, and cling to the thwarts and trust to be soon righted; and (2) a boat which will upset only under strongest pressure, but the men can either stop inside, or if cast out can cling to the keel.

To decide between the merits of these lifeboats would require actual experiment outside and inside of each by the judge, who ought to look at all sides of the question; but my opinion is, at present, in favour of the side-chamber plan, for ships' boats, and of course for steam launches; while the evidence in favour of the other plan for pure lifeboat service in rough water is convincing.

Whatever may be finally settled as to the best position of the air-cases in lifeboats—and the best men in the world for these matters are engaged in earnest upon the subject*—it certainly is prudent for all who care not to be drowned, that the boat they sail in should be so built as not to go down bodily when a mere hole is knocked in her, and this may be insured by dividing her into water-tight compartments.

Some years ago I had a sharp lesson on this point. It was in Dublin Bay, where I was sailing entirely alone in an iron cutter-yacht, very small, yet far too large to

* A foreign sailor, examined as to a shipwreck case in Court, was asked, "How did you know it was the coast of England?" He said, "Because a lifeboat came out to us." Rule Britannia!

be managed by me, then a boy. The throat parrell suddenly broke, and the mainsail jammed at once, so that she would not stay. Then I tried to wear ship, but the running sea poured in over the counter at each plunge, and baling was impossible, for it ran fore and aft. As the water got deeper inside she settled down, for she had no compartments, and being of iron, of course she must speedily sink. A yacht had humanely come out, seeing my distress, and she rounded to and dropped a boy on board me with a strong rope; but when the boy set foot on my bows they plunged deep under water, and with a loud cry he hauled himself back on board the other yacht.

The captain instantly tacked and came again, and cast the rope to me, which I fastened securely to my mast, and then got safely aboard the preserver's vessel, while mine sunk down, but suspended still by the rope, until we towed it into shallow water.

This sort of thing was fully provided against in the *Rob Roy* by the water-tight compartments, three in number, besides the air-chambers, so that if she was filled in any one, she could yet sail on, and if all three compartments had been entirely full of water, she would still float with her air-chambers, and with five hundred-weight to spare.*

The buoyancy of the yawl was very remarkable. She easily carried twenty men, and in the same space one could accommodate five ladies (of the pattern 1866).

A boat's mop is, of course, well known to be always fair spoil to him who can take it, and whatever other article the yachtsman leaves loose on an unguarded

* Three hundredweight of ballast was thrown off at Cowes, beside what we took out at Dover, and still the yawl was stiff.

deck, he never omits to hide or lock up the mop, for a mop is winged like an umbrella, it strays, but seldom returns. The usual protection of mops is their extreme badness, and it is on this account, no doubt, that you never can find a good mop to buy. The *Rob Roy*'s mop was the only bad article on board, and I left it out loose in perfect confidence. Often and often it had evidently been turned over, but on examination it was found supremely bad, worse than the thief's own mop, and not worth stealing. At last, however, and in Cowes, too, the focus of yachting, if not of honesty, my mop was stolen. The man who took it is to be pitied, for, clearly, before he coveted a bad mop, he must have been long enduring a worse one.

Nor is the property in boats' anchors quite free from the legal subtleties which allow but a dim sort of ownership in things that are "attached to the soil."

When, indeed, your boat is at one end of the cable, you will scarcely fear that the anchor should be stolen from the other end. But when necessity or convenience causes you to slip anchor and sail away, you must recollect that though the anchor is the emblem of hope, it does not warrant any *expectation* that on returning you will find the anchor acknowledged to be yours. It has now passed into the category of "found anchors," and it is not yet decided how the rights to these are best determined. However, I may here mention one mode of settling the matter.

A gentleman we shall call N., sailing from a port on the Thames, had to slip his anchor, and he said to the lad ashore—"You see I am leaving my anchor here, and be good enough to tell your father to get it when the tide falls, and to carry it to where my yacht is, and when I return here to-morrow I will give him half-a-crown."

After his sailing was over, N. came back and said to the father, "Well, have you got my anchor?" "I have found an anchor," he answered. "Yes, that is mine, and I told your son I would give you half-a-crown if you brought it here." "I have found an anchor, and I'll not give it up under five shillings," said the man; and their argument and remonstrance gradually enveloped the subject in a hazy abstruseness, while the usual knot of idlers listened all round. At length N. said, "Come, now, we really must settle this matter. I'll *fight you* as to whether I am to pay five shillings or nothing for the anchor," and he took off his coat and waistcoat, so it was plain he was in earnest. The other man stripped too, a ring was formed, and after N., worsted at first, had well thrashed his opponent, the latter gave up the anchor. Here, perhaps, we might think the case had ended, but N. had still a point to be settled, saying to the man, "Your bargain was not only to give up the anchor, but to *bring it here*"; and as the fellow refused to do this, the valiant N. cut the second discussion short by saying, "Well, then, I'll fight you again as to who shall carry it up," and it need scarcely be said that the anchor was not carried up by N.

Is there any other country but England where two men can pummel each other in hard earnest, and yet with less passion at the time, and less grudge afterwards than often exists for years between two combatants who battle with their tongues, or even fight with their pens and post-stamps?

As anchors are important parts of one's equipment,

I had begun early to experiment at once with mine, and the small one had been tried once as a kedge. With the first heave it broke off short; the stock had snapped in the place which ought to be the strongest, but which is really made the weakest, by the present faulty construction of anchor-stocks. The *memo* in my log-book was, "Invent a proper anchor"; and even at Cowes I could not find any plan that met this need.*

Before the end of my voyage, a score of minutiæ, as well as things of some importance, were marked as lines for great improvement, when a nautico-mechanical brain shall be brought to bear upon them. The mental consideration of such points afforded varied subjects for many weeks' thought. Indeed *all* the fittings of a sailing-boat seem open to much improvement. Meanwhile we have laid down the large Trotman as moorings in the Medina, while we range about the bays of the island with the smaller anchor duly repaired.

Of course the dingey had its Sunday voyage at Cowes, and was everywhere received with kindness. It went to the Royal Yacht here, as it had done to the Emperor's yacht at St. Cloud, and the sailors were grateful for books to read, for they have plenty of time on Sundays.

It did not appear to be the fashion at Cowes to work the crews for pleasure sailing seven days a week; indeed, we saw only one yacht sail in on Sunday, and she was arriving after a night's voyage.

* Other inventors, knowing the experimental turn of my crew, had sent me several instruments and things of various sorts to try in practice, and to report on. One of these was a beautiful little anchor made of bronze, and in form very peculiar and apparently an improvement, indeed an admirable novelty to look at. This, too, I heaved overboard for trial, but it simply dragged through the soft mud, and proved quite useless.

CHAPTER XIV

THE *Nonpareil* American life-raft was in Cowes after her
Atlantic voyage of forty-three days at sea. Two of her
three adventurous crew were Prussians, who could speak
English only imperfectly, and the third was a Yankee.
This uncomfortable voyage was undertaken partly to
promote the sale in England of these rafts, and partly
to pay the three men by fees from visitors, while they
could see Europe themselves at a cheap rate. One of
Mr. White's steamers towed the raft in front of the
"Castle," where the members of the Royal Yacht
Squadron Club have their spacious house, with a sea
wall over the waves.

She is schooner-rigged, and very coarsely rigged too.
Gigantic flags and streamers overwhelm her masts, but
fourteen of us on her deck seemed to sink the buoyant
life-raft only an inch more in the water.

She is made of three long tubes of india-rubber blown
up by bellows; and when the air is out, these can be
packed away snugly, weighing in all about a ton, and
intended to be inflated and launched from a ship's deck
in case of disaster. A small raft in the capacity of a
dingey, but formed like the other, was towed beside
her, and as a special favour I was allowed to go away in
this, which was easily worked by oars or sculls upon
outriggers.

The men had for shelter during their long voyage
only a small waterproof tent on the deck, with a gutter

round its edge to catch the rain-water, and so to re-
plenish their supply, kept in bags on each side, and now
handed about in glasses as "travelled liquor," to wash
down biscuits, still surplus from the "sea store." Their
cooking apparatus was at first worked by petroleum, but
this speedily burned the metal out, and they were
driven to manufacture a very ramshackle sort of oil-
lamp, fed by the oil for their ship-light and their compass, and some supplied by passing vessels.

Two centre-boards, like narrow long doors, placed
diagonally between the web joinings of the tubes,
dipped into the water, and served as a keel, so that
when we cast her off from the steamer, the raft managed
to sail a little over to windward. The whole being
collapsible when the air is driven out, can be readily
carried aboard ship, and for this it is valuable, as
is fully explained in the *Lifeboat Journal* for January,
1868.

The actual *substratum*, or raft proper, seems to be
strong and substantial, but the sails and gear were
miserably contrived, and worse executed in preparation
for a long dreary voyage of six weeks, drifting in wet and
weariness, which I could not but contrast with the
pleasant six weeks just passed in the *Rob Roy*.

The most interesting thing on the raft was a passenger,
who had come on board her about a thousand miles
away in the sea. This was an old hen, given to the crew
by a passing vessel. It was a common brown, dowdy,
grandmother-looking hen, and in this prosaic state it
was very odd and incongruous, tethered to the deck by
a bit of tarred lanyard, and pecking away till you
looked hard at it, then it cocked up one eye with an air
that said, "Why are you staring at *me*?"

Among the visitors to the raft was a wealthy gentleman, who surveyed the whole with interest, and at last
fixed his eye upon the barn-door fowl, and asked if it
was to be sold. "Yes, sir, for a hundred guineas," was
the answer; but he deferred any immediate purchase by
saying, "If I thought that eating that hen's eggs would
make me as plucky as you are, I might buy it." As for
being "plucky" in the matter, what will not men risk
for money? The risks run by many sailors in the rotten
coffins that bring our scuttles of coals round Yarmouth
Sands are quite as great as the hazard on this raft, and
their forecastles are about as comfortable as the tent
upon it. If it were not on such a serious subject as risk
to human life, one might well be amused to hear the
wrong estimates of the dangers in various sorts of
voyages which are so hastily expressed by benevolent
people who are ignorant of the whole matter.

I advised the raft-men to take her to Berlin, for
exhibition as "the Prussian raft from America," for
such she is; but they persisted in their scheme for showing her in London, where folks are already tired of
"flotsam and jetsam" from the West. Their enterprise
failed; and the poor Prussians had to depart from
England deep in debt instead of laden with money, and
their raft was left for sale.

Since the *Nonpareil*, there has come to England from
America, the (let us hope) last floating monstrosity, a
boat called the *John T. Ford*, worse "found" in every
sense than the others, with three men drowned on the
passage, and one nearly starved—a sad finale to the
failures of the *Henrietta, Red, White, and Blue,* and *Nonpareil,* as speculations. Perhaps, for a time at least, the
Americans will be cautious how they exhibit their boats

for sale here, when the principal characteristic of each of them is the sensational foolhardiness of the crew.

Every day at Cowes the yawl *Rob Roy* was under way for a sail, and sometimes in good breezes she would thread in and out among thickly clustered yachts, so as to show her handiness. Certainly, without previous practice, it would be highly improper to attempt this sort of cruising; for the yachts, with bowsprits run out, and jiggers and mizen-booms projecting, are at anchor here on the implied understanding that no one will wantonly endanger a collision by sailing about in the crowd, merely for fun. After practice, however, for weeks in the same craft, the operation of guiding her safely through a maze of boats, and on a strong cross-tide, becomes like the unnoticed and nearly involuntary muscular efforts of the body which carry us safely through a crowd on shore. I recollect once seeing some very dignified Arab Chiefs, who for the first time in their lives had to go upstairs, and their awkward stumbling, even in the ascent of a few steps, showed how much our nerves and limbs have to learn before we can do so ordinary a thing without even a thought.

One day the *Rob Roy* sailed to Portsmouth, and into all the creeks and crannies, and through all the channels and guts she could find in that complicated waterway, and then anchored near the *Duke of Wellington*, with the old *Victory* close beside. There also was the *Serapis*, the new and magnificent troop-ship, of a size and build found to be the best success of our last naval efforts. By the quay was the *Warrior*, the first sea-going iron-clad, and of beauty indisputable, and the celebrated *Wyvern*, with its tripod masts. Others later made, and always more and more stumpy and square, need a strong pressure of utilitarian conviction to restrain us from pronouncing that they are downright ugly. But we shall soon become reconciled, and then enamoured, of forms that are associated with proved utility, and the grand three-decker of our youth will look as clumsy then as the ships of Queen Elizabeth do now, which seem to have carried, each of them, a lot of toy guns, and a country mansion on its deck.

The church service on board old *Victory* was most interesting to take part in when Sunday came round, and next day her captain came to visit us in his well-manned gig, which, indeed, was longer than our boat, and he said that the *Rob Roy* "fulfilled a dream of his youth." This from a "swell of the ocean" was a high compliment to our little yawl.

A boat full of boys, from the Portsmouth Ragged School, sang hymns on the water in the lovely evening.

.   .   .   .

CHAPTER XV

Cowes Regatta days opened with wind and rain; but even at the best of times the sight of a sailing-match from on shore is like that of a stag hunt from on foot— very pretty at the start, and then very little more to see. It is different if you sail about among the competing yachts. Then you feel the same tide and wind, and see the same marks and buoys, and dread the same shoals and rocks as they do, and at every turn of every vessel you have something to learn.

No one can satisfactorily distribute the verdict "victor" or "vanquished" in a sailing-match between the designer, the builder, the rigger, and the course, the weather, the rules, the sailor of each craft, and chance; though each of these will conduce in part to the success or failure in every match. Still there is this advantage, that the loser can always blame, and the winner can always praise, which of these elements he finds most convenient. But if a sailing-match has little in it quite intelligible, even when you see it, the account of a past regatta is well worth keeping out of print—so be it then with this one, the best held at Cowes for many years.

. . . .

The "voyage alone" had culminated at Cowes when the splendid exhibition of fireworks closed the grand show of British yachting. It was a beautiful sight those whizzing rockets speeding from wave to sky, and scattering bright gems above to fall softly from the black heaven; those glares of red or green that painted all the wide crescent of beauteous hulls, and dim, tall masts with a glow of ardent colour, and the "bouquets" of fantastic form and hue, with noise that rattled aloft, while thousands of paled faces cheered loud below. To this day the deck of the *Rob Roy* bears marks of the fire-shower falling quietly, gently down, but still with a red scar burned in black at the last.

Luggage is all on board again, and our "Blue Peter" flies at the fore, for the *Rob Roy* will weigh anchor now for her homeward voyage. The Ryde Regatta was well worth seeing, and she stopped there in an uneasy night, but we need not copy the log of another set of sailing-matches.

Thus in a fine evening, when the sun sunk ruddy and the breeze blew soft, we turned again to Brading harbour, and, just perhaps because we had come safely once before, there was listless incaution now, as if Bembridge reef could not be cruel on such a fine evening as this.

Various and doubtless most true directions had been given to me as to entering this narrow channel: "Keep the tree in a line with the monument; that's your mark." But when you come there and see the monument, there are twenty trees; and which then is *the* tree to guide by? Here, therefore, and in mundane things on land too it is alike, the misapprehension of a rule was worse than the chance mistake of undirected motherwit. A horrid crash brought us suddenly to rest; the *Rob Roy* had struck on a rock. Though I was lax at the time, and lolling and lazy, yet presence of mind remained. Down

L 161

came the sails, out leaped the anchor, and shoving, and hauling, and rowing did their best; but no, she was firmly berthed on one of the north-west rocks. Presently a malicious wave lifted her stern round, and the rudder soon bumped on another sharp ledge, until by sounding and patience I at last got her free, and rowed out through a channel unconscionably narrow, and then ran the sails up, and the yawl was safe again, sailing smoothly, with a deep sigh of deliverance.

A sailing-boat had put off from the shore to help, seeing the catastrophe, but I signalled to her, "Thanks —all right now," and she went back. Soon another boat that had rowed out came near, and the man in her determined to be a *salvor*, whether or no, and leaped on board the yawl. I made him get off to his boat; I had not invited him, nor had he asked permission to board me. He could see it was the other man's job, and he ought to have obeyed the signal, as did the other. Grumbling heavily, he at length asked me to tow him in. "Well," I said, "why, yes, I will give you a tow, though you have been very impudent." But the moment he came near he jumped on board again, resolved to save me, though I might protest ever so hard. Once more, then, I bundled him into his boat, and this time rather by deeds than words. He kept up a volley of abuse all the way to the shore, and there I gave my yawl in charge of the first man, who had acted right both in coming out and in going back when signalled. A hospitable Captain R.N. offered me his moorings (as good as a bed for a boat), and asked me to breakfast next day, which was accepted, "subject to wind," especially as he was of the clan "Mac," like his guest.

Calm night falls on the *Rob Roy*, in a little inland lake,

profoundly still, more quiet, indeed, in respect of current, tide, or wind, or human being, than any night of the voyage. It was very difficult to turn in below with such a moon above, and water quite unruffled. So there was a long lean-to on propped elbows, and reverie reeled off by the yard.

Daybreak grey, with a westerly breeze, at once dissolved the breakfast engagement, and carried the *Rob Roy* to sea, with her own kettle briskly boiling; and now we are fairly started on our voyage to the Thames again. But the glowing sun also took its morning meal, and greedily ate up the wind; and so the yachts from Ryde could be seen far off, looking farther off in a misty curtain, all only drifting with the tide, while they raced their hardest for a cup. Yet there is science and skill in drifting well. If the skipper has no wind to show his prowess in with sails, he must win by his knowledge of current, tide, and channel, while he seems perhaps to be carried along helplessly. One after another the pretty racers slowly rounded the Warner lightship, and then each sunk back, as it were, into the gauzy distance, until they seemed like white pearls dotted on grey satin, and the *Rob Roy* was alone again, while the fog thickened more. Land was shut out, then sky, then every single thing, and the glazed sea seemed to stiffen as if it had set flat and smooth for ever.

To know that this state of things was to last for hours would make it intolerable, but the expectancy of every moment buoys up the mind in hope, and every past moment is buried as you reach thus forward to the next coming.

Then the inexorable tide turned dead against me, and down went my anchor; for, at any rate, we must not be floated backwards. Tool-chest opened, and hammer and saw are instantly at work, for there are still "things to be done" on board, and when all improvements shall have been completed then vacant hours like these will be tedious enough; but never fear, there is no finality in a sailing-boat, if the brain keeps inventing and the fingers respond.

Out of the thick creamy fog a huge object slowly loomed, with a grand air of majesty, and a low but strenuous sound as it came nearer and clearer to eye and ear. It was an enormous Atlantic steamer, and it went circling round and round in ample bends, but never too far to be unexpected again. Sometimes her great paddles moved with a measured plash, but slow, until she dissolved before my eyes into a faded vision. Again, when hidden, there would still come a deep moaning from her hoarse fog-whistle out of the impenetrable whiteness, and she again towered up suddenly behind, ever wheeling, gliding on vapour and water so commingled that you could not say she floated, but was somehow faintly present like the dim picture on a canvas screen from a magic lantern half in focus. She was searching in the fog for the "Nab" lightship, thence to take new bearings and cleave the mist in a straight course at half-speed for Southampton. When she found the "Nab" she vanished finally, and I was glad and sorry she was gone.

After long waiting, the faintest zephyr now at last dallied with my light flag for a minute, and the anchor was instantly raised. A schooner, also outward bound, soon slowly burst its way through the cloudy barrier, and I tried to follow her, but she, too, melted into dimness, and left me in a noiseless, sightless vacancy, except when the distant gong of the lightship told that they also had a fog there.

How did the ancients by any possibility manage to sail in a fog without a compass? In those days, too, they had no charts; yes, and there was no "Wreck chart," to tell at the year's end all the havoc strewn at the bottom of the sea.

Well we sailed on, and on, always seeming to sail on into pure cotton-wool, which blushed a little with an evening tint as the sun tired down, and so here was a long day told off and ending; but where exactly am I now as darkness falls?

You will say, "Why, the chart tells that, of course"; and so it does, if you have anything like sure reckoning to indicate what part of the mazy groups of figures on it to look for as your probable place; otherwise a dozen different places in it will all suit your soundings, and eleven of them are wrong.

Consider the *data* for our calculation. The *Rob Roy* had been carried by two tides; one this way, the other that. She had sailed on three different tacks, that is, in various angular directions, and with different speeds, and these complicating forces had acted for times very uncertain. Where is she now? an all-important question for settling the start-point in a night cruise, and on a dangerous coast.

The last time I was sailing in fog was on the Baltic, in my canoe, where, just at the nick of time, a look-out man was descried on a high ladder far overlooking the low rocky islands of the Swedish coast, and he speedily showed me that my bow was then pointed exactly wrong for the desired haven.

This may be the time, perhaps, to compare the canoe

voyage with the yawl cruise, even if we cannot settle the question so often put to me, "Which was the most agreeable?"

A canoe voyage can be enjoyed by several men, each in a separate boat, and yet all in a combined party; that is, with distinct responsibility but united companionship. The yawl cruise devolves both toil and care on one alone, but he also has all the pleasure, and so it might be pronounced at once to be more *selfish* than the other voyage. But after a score of tours, in large and small parties, I see that selfishness is quite independent of the number concerned. A man who is pleasing his wife or his children in a tour I do not count at all; for everything that delights or benefits *them* is, of course, a pleasure to *him*. Or again, he may journey with ten companions, and his travelling circle will indeed be larger, but the centre of it may be after all the same.

Of the thousand tourists who rush out over the Continent each summer there is little check on selfishness by meeting people in trains, steamers, and hotels for a temporary acquaintance, which is speedily dissolved as soon as the interests or the likings of the companions are not coincident.

Unselfishness appears to consist in doing good when it is not exactly pleasant to do it, and to people who are not in our own groove, or in "our set," but like the people invited in the feast prescribed by Christ, and for whom we work as a duty, whether it is immediately agreeable or not. It is giving up our own will to God's command, and obeying this ungrudgingly; and yet our own pleasure may be most in giving others pleasure, and we can be lavish of labour for others while selfish at the core. Thus it seems to be very difficult ever to be unselfish in the sense that it is often absurdly insisted upon; namely, that others are everything and yourself nothing. Nevertheless, after all casuistry, we know what is *meant* by "selfish," as an undue regard. But the result of an action is to be looked at, and it does not become selfish because we do one part of it alone. A man who steps out from a crowd to pluck flowers alone on the edge of the cliff may bring back a bouquet that will give fragrant pleasure to them all, while another who stays in the group of gatherers may gather none at all or may be very selfish about his handful. Our lonely labour may, in fact, be most of all useful for other people in the end.

The anxieties of the canoe trip are more varied and less heavy than in a sailing cruise.

In the yawl I was always sure of food and lodging, but then in the canoe one does not fear wind, wave, calm, and fog; for, at any rate, one can at the worst take the canoe ashore. The risk of a total loss of the canoe is only fifteen pounds gone, but the other shipwreck risks ten times as much, and whereas each canoe danger can usually be avoided, those met in sailing at sea are often to be encountered without any escape.

The physical endurance required in a canoe is more under control of a previous arrangement. The muscular exertion with the paddle is generally voluntary, while that in the yawl was often hardest when one wanted most to rest. You need scarcely be forced, in canoeing, to go on two days and two nights without sleep, as will be seen was the fate in the yawl.

The scenery in traversing land and water in a canoe is, of course, more varied than in sailing always at sea, but the perils of the deep have a grandeur and wideness that seem to rouse far more the inner soul, and with more profound emotions. The thoughts during a night storm at sea are of a higher strain than those in passing the rapids in a river.

Finally, there is at first a sense of incongruity in the appearance of a canoe when in a cart, on a train, or in a house, and you have often to meet an inexplicable but evident *smile* at the whole affair, which perhaps comes from pity, certainly from ignorance, and it may be from contempt; whereas a sailing-boat crossing the deep is doing what people in ports and ships know very well about, and if your boat keeps on doing it successfully they cannot despise the deed because the boat that does it is small. A man who comes to the "meet" on a little pony will not be laughed at if he is always well in at the death.

. . . .

CHAPTER XVI

"WHERE is the yawl now?" was the question we had asked in the fog, and the natural answer was—that the chart would tell, of course. So let us look at the small slice of chart copied on p. 173. It is crammed, you see, with figures of soundings, and names of banks, buoys, and beacons; but the only thing to be seen on the actual horizon around us, is the Owers light behind, and about N.W. in its bearing. The tide will soon turn against our progress towards the east, therefore we tack towards shore, so as to be within anchorage soundings should it become needful to stop, for the wind has just changed rather suspiciously, and we can even hear the sound of the drums at Portsmouth as they beat the taptoo. A few bright meteors shoot athwart the heavens above, reminding us that this is one of their usual epochs—the 14th of August.

Now we are in ten fathoms by the lead, and we must anchor here, for the tide has fully turned and the wind has lulled, and perhaps it will do to sleep for six hours here before going on again.

The beautiful phosphorescence of the sea on this occasion was an attractive sight, and I could follow the line of my hemp cable by the gleam of silver light which enfolded it with a gradually softened radiance from the surface of the sea, down—down to an unseen depth, where, in sooth, it was dark enough.*

The gentle motion of riding with a chain-cable is quite in contrast to that when anchored by a rope; for this latter will jerk and pull, while the heavier chain, laid in a drooping curve, acts as a constant spring that eases and cushions every rude blow.

I intended to start again with any freshening breeze, and to get into Littlehampton for the night; therefore the small anchor and the hemp cable were used so as to be more ready for instant departure, and well it was thus.

Time sped slowly between looking at my watch to know the tide change, and dozing as I lay in the cabin— the dingey being, of course, astern; until in the middle of the night, lapsing through many dreams, I had glided into that delicious state when you dream that you are dreaming. On a sudden, and without any seeming cause, I felt perfectly awake, and yet in a sort of a trance, and lying still a time, seeking what could possibly have awakened me thus. Then there came through the dark a peal of thunder, long, and loud, and glorious.

How changed the scene to look upon! No light to be seen from the Owers now, but a flash from above and then darkness, and soon a grand rolling of the same majestic, deep-toned roar.

Now I must prepare for wind. On with the life-belt,

* To anchor for the night, riding by tide or stream, is not pleasant; for then the wind may cross your hatch, and blow the rain in sideways, whereas if you ride at anchor to the wind alone, the draught comes always from the front, and so it can be better provided for, and the boat does not roll much even if she pitches.

close the hatches, loose the mainsail, and double reef it, and reef the jib. Off with the mizen and set the storm-sail, and now haul up the anchor while yet there is time; and there was scarcely time before a rattling breeze got up, and waves rose too, and rain came down as we sailed off south to the open sea for room. Sea room is the sailor's want: the land is what he fears more than the water.

We were soon fast spinning along, and the breeze brushed the haze all away, but the night was very dark, and the rain made it hard to see. Now and then the thunder swallowed all other sounds, as the cries of the desert are silenced by the lion's roar.

Sometimes there was an arch shining above as the flashes leaped across the upper clouds, and then a sharp upright prong of forked lightning darted straight down between, while rain was driven along by the wind, and salt foam dashed up from the waves. It seemed like an earthly version of that heavenly vision which was beheld in Patmos by the beloved John: "And I heard as it were the voice of a great multitude, and as the voice of many waters, and as the voice of mighty thunderings."*

How well our English word "thunder" suits the meaning in its sound, far better than *tonnerre* or *tonitru*.

In the dark, a cutter dashed by me, crossing the yawl's bows, just as the lightning played on us both. It had no ship-light up, shameful to say. I shouted out, "Going south?" and they answered, "Yes; come along off that shore."

From the bit of chart here copied (covering only a few miles) it will be understood what kind of shore we had

* Revelation, xix. 6.

to avoid. There was quite water enough for our shallow craft, but it was the twisting of currents and tides that made the danger here.

The breeze now turned west, then south, and every other way, and it was exceedingly perplexing to know at once what to do in each case, especially as the waves became short and snappish under this pressure from different sides, and yet my compass quietly pointed right, with a soft radiance shining from it, and my mast-light in a brighter glow gleamed from behind me* on the white crests of the waves.

At one time a heavy squall roughened the dark water, and taxed all my powers to work the little yawl; but whenever a lull came or a chance of getting on my proper course again, I bent round to "East by North," determined to make way in that direction.

In the middle of the night my compass lamp began to glimmer faint, and it was soon evident that the flame must go out. Here was a discomfort: the wind veered so much that its direction would be utterly fallacious as a guide to steer by, and this uncertainty might continue until the lightning ceased. Therefore, at all hazards, we must light up the compass again. So I took down the ship-light from the mizen shroud, and held it between my knees that it might shine on the needle, and it was curious how much warmth came from this lantern. Then I managed to get a candle, and cut a piece off, and rigged it up with paper inside the binnacle. This answered for about ten minutes, but finding it was again flickering, I opened the tin door, and found all the candle had melted into bright liquid oil; so this

* It was hung on the port mizen shroud. To hang it in front of you is simply to cut off two of your three chances of possibly seeing ahead.

THE OWERS.

0   1   2 MILES.

Pagham

Earnley   Pagham Harb.

Selsea Ho.

Thorney C.G.

C.G.

Hounds dry at L.W.

Selsea Street C.G.

Selsea Bill

MEDMERY BK.   Streets

Grounds

Dries

Cheq.

Beacon

The Mixon dry at L.W.

Brake or Cross Ledge

Pullar Bed

THE LOOE

Boulder Bank

Van.

Pillar

Bank

MIDDLE OWERS

MAGNETIC

makeshift was a failure. However, another candle was cut, and the door being left open to keep it cool, with this lame light I worked on bravely, but very determined for the rest of my sailing days to have the oil bottle always accessible. Finally, the wind blew out the candle, though it was very much sheltered, and the ship-light almost at the same time also went out suddenly. Then we lay to, backed the jib, opened the cabin hatch, got out the oil, thoroughly cleaned the lamp, put in a new wick, and lighted it afresh, and a new candle in the ship's light; then we started all right once more, with that self-gratulation at doing all this successfully, under such circumstances of wind, sea, and rain, which perhaps was not more than due.

What with these things, and reefing several times, and cooking at intervals, there was so much to do and so much to think about during the night, that the hours passed quickly, and at last some stray streaks of dawn (escaped before their time perhaps) lighted up a cloud or two above, and then a few wave-tops below, and soon gave a general grey tint to all around, until by imperceptible but sure advance of clearness, the vague horizon seemed to split into land and water, and happily then it was seen plainly that the *Rob Roy* had not lost way in the dark.

As soon as there was light enough to read we began to study Shoreham in the Pilot-book, and neared it the while in the water; but though now opposite the Brighton coast, it was yet too far away to make out any town, for we had stood well out to sea in the thunderstorm. All tiredness passed off with the fresh morning air, and the breeze was now so strong that progress was steady and swift.

THE YAWL ROB ROY

It may be remarked how a coast often appears quite different when you are fifteen or twenty miles out at sea, from what it does when you stand on the beach, or look from a row-boat close to the land. So now we were puzzled to find out Brighton, one's own familiar Brighton, with its dull half-sided street, neither town nor bathing-town, its beach unwalkable, and all its sights and glories done in a day. We might well be ashamed not to recognize at once the contour of the hills, so often trudged over in square or in skirmish in the Volunteer Reviews.

The chain-pier was, of course, hardly discernible at a great distance. But the "Grand Hotel" at last asserted itself as a black cubical speck in the binocular field, and then we made straight for that; Shoreham being gradually voted a bore to be passed by, and Newhaven adopted as the new goal for the day.

We had shaken out all reefs, and now tore along at full speed, with the spray-drift sparkling in the sun, and a frolicsome jubilant sea. The delights of going fast when the water is deep and the wind is strong—ah! these never can be rightly described, nor the exulting bound with which your vessel springs through a buoyant wave, and the thrill of nerve that tells in the sailor's heart, "Well, after all, sailing is a pleasure supreme."

Numerous fishing-vessels now came out, with their black tanned sails and strong bluff bows and hardy-looking crews, who all hailed me cheerily when they were near enough, and often came near to see. Fast the yawl sped along the white chalk cliffs, and my chart in its glazed frame did excellent service now, for the wind and sea rose more again; and at length, when we came near the last headland for Newhaven, we lowered the

mainsail and steadily ran under mizen and jib. Newhaven came in sight, deeply embayed under the magnificent cliff, which at other times I could have gazed
on for an hour, admiring the grand dashing of the
waves, but we had to hoist mainsail again, so as to get
in before the tide would set out strongly, and increase
the sea at the harbour's mouth every minute.

It was more than exciting to enter here with such
waves running. Rain, too, came on, just as the *Rob Roy*
dashed into the first three rollers, and they were big and
green, and washed her well from stem right on to stern,
but none entered further. The bright yellow hue of the
waves on one side of the pier made me half-afraid that it
was shallow there, and hesitating to pass I signalled to
some men near the pier-head as to which way to go,
but they were only visitors. The tide ran strongly out,
dead in my teeth, yet the wind took me powerfully
through it all, and then instantly, even before we had
rounded into quiet water, the inquisitive uncommunica-
tive spectators roared out, "Where are you from?"
"What's your name?" and all such stupid things to say
to a man whose whole mind in a time like this has to be
on sail and sea and tiller.*

During this passage from the Isle of Wight I had
noticed now and then when the waves tossed more than
usual, that a dull, heavy, thumping sound was heard
aboard the yawl, and gradually I concluded that her
iron keel had been broken by the rock at Bembridge,
and that it was swinging free below my boat. This idea

* I think that in a port like Newhaven the look-out man in
charge ought to come to the pier-head when he sees a yacht
entering in rough weather, and certainly there is more attention
to such matters in France than with us.

increased my anxiety to get in safely; and to make sure of the matter we took the *Rob Roy* at once to the "gridiron," and laid her alongside a screw-steamer which had been out during the night, and had run on a rock in the dark thunderstorm. The "baulks" or beams of the gridiron under water were very far apart, and we had much difficulty in placing the yawl so as to settle down on two of them, but the crew of the steamer helped me well, and all the more readily, as I had given them books at Dieppe, a gift they did not now forget.

Just as the ebbing tide had lowered the yawl fairly on the baulks, another steamer came in from France, crowded with passengers, and the waves of her swell lifted my poor little boat off her position, and rudely fixed her upon only one baulk, from which it was not possible to move her; therefore, when the tide descended she was hung up askew in a ludicrous position of extreme discomfort to her weary bones; but when I went outside to examine below, there was nothing whatever amiss, and gladness for this outweighed all other troubles, and left me quite ready for a good sleep at night.

For this purpose we rowed the yawl into a quiet little river, and lashed her alongside a neat schooner, whose captain and wife and children and their little dog "Lady" were soon great friends, for they were courteous people, as might be expected in a respectable vessel; it is generally so.

Now the *Rob Roy* settled into soft mud for a good rest of three days, and I went to the Inn where Mr. Smith landed from France in 1848, after he had given up being Louis Philippe.

The Inn trades upon this fact, and it has other peculiarities—very bad chops, worse tea, no public room, and a very deaf waitress! the whole sufficiently uncomfortable to justify my complaint, and it must be a very bad inn indeed that is not comfortable enough for *me*.

Here I was soon accosted by a reader of canoe books, and next day we inspected the oyster-beds, and a curious corn-mill driven by tide-water, confined in a basin—one of the few mills worked by the power of the moon. Also we wandered over the new sea fortifications, which are built and hewed by our Government one week, and the week afterwards if there comes a shower of rain they tumble down again. This is the case, at any rate, with the Newhaven fortress, and we must only hope that an invading army will not attack the place during the wrong week.

Three steamers in a day, all crowded with Exhibition passengers, that was a large traffic for a small port like Newhaven; but it did not raise the price of anything except ham sandwiches, and I bought my supplies of eggs and butter and bread, and walked off with them all, as usual, to the extreme astonishment of an aristocratic shop-woman.

In crossing a viaduct my straw hat blew off into a deep hole among mud, and I asked a boy to fetch it. The little fellow was a true Briton. He put down his bundle, laboriously built a bridge of stones, and at imminent risk of a regular mud-bath, at length clasped the hat. His pluck was so admirable, that he had a shilling as a reward, which, be it observed, was half the price of the hat itself two months before, a "No. 2" hat, useful to shop in.

This incident put an end to quiet repose, for the boy-life of the town was soon stirred to its lowest depth, and

178

all youngsters with any spirit of gain trooped down to
the yawl, waiting off and on for the next day also, in
hopes of another mishap as a chance of luck to them.

The dingey, too, had its usual meed of applause;
but one rough mariner was so vociferous in deriding its
minuteness, that at last I promised him a sovereign if
he could catch me, and he might take any boat in the
port. At first he was all for the match, and began to
strip and prepare, but his ardour cooled, and his abuse
also subsided.

Many Colchester boats were here, nearly all of them
well found, and with civil crews, who were exceedingly
grateful for books to read on the Sunday, and resting
among them was a little yacht of five tons, which had
been sent out with only one man to take her from Dover
to Ryde. Poor fellow! he had lost his way at night and
was unable to keep awake, until at last two fishermen
fell in with the derelict and brought him in here,
hungry and amazed; but I regarded him with a good
deal of interest as rather in my line of life, and I quite
understood his drowsy feelings when staring at the
compass in the black, whistling rain.

CHAPTER XVII

THE barometer mounted steadily all Sunday, so we
resolved to start next morning at break of day. But
though the night was quiet, the vessels near my berth
were also getting ready, therefore at last I gave up all
hopes of sleep, and for company's sake got ready also
after midnight, that we might have all the tide possible
for going round Beachy Head, which, once passed, we
could find easy ports all the way to London. So about
two o'clock, in the dark, we are rowing out again
on the ebbing tide, and the water at the pier-head
looks placid now compared with the boiling and dashing
it made there when the yawl passed in before.

Dawn broke an hour afterwards with a dank and
silent mist skirting up far-away hills, and a gentle east
wind faintly breathing as our tea-cup smoked fragrant
on deck. The young breeze was only playful yet, so we
anchored, waiting for it to rise in earnest or the tide to
slacken, as both of them were now contrary; and meantime we rested some hours preparing for a long spell of
unknown work; but I could not sleep in such a lovely
daybreak, not having that most valuable capacity of
being able to sleep when it is wanted for coming work,
and not for labour past.

The east wind baffled the yawl and a whole fleet of
vessels, all of us trying to do the same thing, namely, to
arrive at Beachy Head before two o'clock in the day;

for, if this could be managed, we should there find the tide ebbing eastwards, and so get twelve hours of current in our favour.

This feature—the division of the tides there—makes Beachy Head a well-marked point in the navigation of the Channel. The stream from the North Sea meets the other from the Atlantic here, and here also they begin to separate. After beating, in downright sailing, one after another of the schooners and brigs and barques in company, I saw at last with real regret that not one of us could reach the point in time, and yet the yawl got there only a few minutes too late; but it was dead calm, and I even rowed her on to gain the last little mile.

One after another the vessels gave it up, and each cast anchor. Coming to a pilot steamer, I hailed: "Shall I be able to do it?" "No, sir," they said; "no—very sorry for you, sir; you've worked hard, sir, but you're ten minutes too late." Within that time the tide had turned against us. We had not crossed the line of division, and so the yawl had to be turned towards shore to anchor there, and to wait the tide until nine o'clock at night, unless a breeze came sooner.

After three hours' work she reached the desired six fathoms' patch of sand, just under the noble white cliff that rears its head aloft about 600 feet, standing ever as a giant wall, sheer, upright, out of the sea.

Dinner done and everything set right (for this is best policy always), I slipped into my cabin and tried to sleep as the sun went down, but a little land-breeze now began, and every now and then my head was raised to see how tide or wind progressed. Then I must have fallen once into a mild nap, and perhaps a dream, for sudden and strong a rough hand seemed to shake the boat, and, on my leaping up, there glanced forth a brilliant flash of lightning that soon put everybody on the *qui vive*.

Now was heard the clink of distant cables, as I raised mine also in the dark, with only the bright shine of the lighthouse like a keen and full-opened eye gazing down from the cliff overhead.

Compass lighted, ship-lantern fixed, a reef in each sail, and, with a moment's thought of the very similar events that had passed only a few nights ago, we steered right south, away, away to the open sea.

It was black enough all around; but yet the strong wind expected after thunder had not come, and we edged away eastward, doubly watchful, however, of the dark, for the crowd of vessels here was the real danger, and not the sea.

The ghost of Rob Roy is flitting on the white sail as the lamp shines brightly. Down comes the rain, and with it flash after flash, peal upon peal of roaring thunder, and the grandeur of the scene is unspeakable. The wind changed every few minutes, and vessels and boats and steamers whirled past like visions, often much too near to be welcome.

A white dazzling gleam of forked lightning cleaves the darkness, and, behold! a huge vessel close at hand, but hitherto unseen, lofty and full-sailed, and for a moment black against the instant of light, and then utterly lost again. The plashing of rain hissed in the sea, and a voice would come out of the unseen—"Port, you lubber!" The ship or whatever it is has no lights at all, though on board it they can see mine. Ah, it's no use peering forward to discover on which side is the new danger; for when your eye has gazed for a time at the lighted compass it is powerless for a minute or two to see in the dark space forward, or, again, if you stare into the blackness to scan the faintest glimmer of a sail ahead, then for some time after you cannot see the compass when looking at it dazzled. This difficulty in sailing alone is the only one we felt to be quite insuperable.

Again a steam whistle shrieked amid the thunder, and two eyes glared out of the formless vapour and rain— the red and the green lights—the signals that showed where she was steaming. There was shouting from her deck as she kept rounding and backing, no doubt for a man overboard. As we slewed to starboard to avoid her, another black form loomed close on the right; and what with wind, rain, thunder, and ships, there was everything to confuse just when there was all need of cool decision.

It would be difficult for me to exaggerate the impressive spectacle that passed along on the dark background of this night. To show what others thought, we may quote the following paragraph from the *Pall Mall Gazette* of next day, August 20:*

The storm which raged in London through the whole of last night was beyond question by far the most severe and protracted which has occurred for many years. It began at half-past eight o'clock, after a day of intense heat, which increased as the evening advanced, though it never reached the sultriness which was remarked before the storm of last week. The first peal of thunder was heard about nine, and from that time till after five this morning it never ceased for more than a few minutes, while the lightning may be said to have been absolutely continuous. Its vivid character

---

* The singular volcanic eruptions in Iceland occurred also this day.

was something quite unusual in the storms of recent summers, and the thunder by which it was often instantaneously followed can only be described as terrific. The storm reached its greatest violence between two and three o'clock, when a smart gale of wind sprang up, and for about ten minutes the tempest was really awful.

We had noticed some rockets sent up from Eastbourne earlier in the evening; probably these were fireworks at a fête there, but the rain must have soon drowned the gala. Certainly it closed up my view of all other lights but the lightning, though sometimes a shining line appeared for a moment in the distance, perhaps from Hastings; and at one time the moon came out red and full, and exactly at the top of a vessel's lofty sails. One steamer had puzzled me much by its keeping nearly still. This drifted close up at last, and they called out, "Ahoy, there!—are you a fishing-boat?" They wanted to know their bearings, as the current and shifting wind made the position of Beachy Head quite uncertain in the dark.* I replied to their hail—"No, I'm the yacht *Rob Roy*, crew of one man; don't you see my white sails?" and they answered—"See? why, who can see to-night?"

Sometimes a sudden and dead lull came with an ominous meaning, and then the loud hissing of rain could be heard advancing to us in the dark till it poured on the yawl in sheets of water, and the mere dripping from the peak of my sou'wester was enough to obscure vision.

And yet, after a few hours of the turmoil and excite-

* The numerous vessels met now were some of those we had been with in the morning, and they looked even more in number, for we crossed and recrossed each other frequently, and this part of the Channel is a highway for nations.

ment, this state of things became quite as if it were natural, so soon does one get accustomed to any circumstances, however strange at first. I even cooked hot tea; it was something to do, as well as to drink, and singing and whistling also beguiled the dark hours of eager, strained watching. In a lighter moment, once a great lumbering sloop sailed near, and we hailed her loudly, "How's the wind going to be?"—for the wind kept ever changing (but the thunder and lightning were going on still). A gruff voice answered, "Can't say; who *can* say—night—this sort—think it'll settle east." This was bad news for me, but it did not come true. The sloop's skipper wished for an east wind, and so he expected it.

A stranger sound than any before now forced attention as it rapidly neared us, and soon the sea was white around with boiling, babbling little waves—what could it be? Instantly I sounded with the lead, but there was no bottom—we were not driving on shore—it was one of the "overfalls" or "ripples" we have mentioned before, where a turbid sea is raised in deep water by some far-down precipice under the waves.

The important question at once arose as to which of the "overfalls" on my chart this could be—the one marked as only a mile from Beachy Head, or the other ten miles further on. Have we been turning and wheeling about all this dreary night in only a few square miles of sea, or have we attained the eastern tide, and so are now running fast on our course?

The incessant and irksome pitching and rolling which the overfalls caused, might be patiently borne, if only we could be assured the yawl progressed. But all was still left in doubt.

So sped the storm for eight long hours, with splendours for the eye, and deep long thrills of the sublime, that stirred deep the whole inner being with feelings vivid and strong and loosed the most secret folds of consciousness with thoughts I had never felt before, and perhaps shall never know again. The mind conjured up the most telling scenes it had known of "alone" and of "thunder," to compare with this where both were now combined.

To stand on the top of Mont Blanc, that round white icicle highest in Europe, and all alone to gaze on a hundred peaks around—that was indeed impressive.

More so was it to kneel alone at the edge of Etna, and to fill the mind from the smoking crater with thoughts and fancies teeming out of the hot, black, and wide abyss.

Thunder and lightning, also, in the crater of Vesuvius we had wondered at before; and it had been grander still, when the flashes lighted up Niagara, pouring out its foam that glistened for a moment dazzling white and then vanished, while the thundering heavens sounded louder than the heavy torrent tumbling into the dark. But here, in my yawl on the sea, was more splendid than these. Imagination painted its own free picture on a black and boundless background of mind strung tight by near danger; and from out this spoke the deep loud diapason, while the quick flashing at intervals gave point to all. Then that glorious anthem came to my memory, where these words of the 18th Psalm are nobly rendered:—

He bowed the heavens and came down, and darkness was under His feet.

He rode upon a cherub and did fly; yea, He did fly upon the wings of the wind.

He made darkness His secret place; the pavilion round about
Him were dark waters and thick clouds of the skies.

The Lord also thundered in the heavens, and the Highest gave
His voice: hail stones and coals of fire.

Then the channels of waters were seen, and the foundations
of the world were discovered: at Thy rebuke, O Lord, at the blast
of the breath of Thy nostrils.

He sent down from above, He took me, He drew me up out of
many waters.

The sensations were prolonged enough to be analysed
and reasoned upon, and it was a difficult question
which cannot yet be answered—"Would I willingly
have all this over again?" Lying on a sofa in a comfortable room, I would not go out to this scene; but in a
boat, if all this began again, I certainly would not go
ashore to avoid its discomforts and lose its grandeurs.

The profound uncertainty as to what was to come
next moment being one of the most exciting features of
the occasion, perhaps the whole scene would be tamed
sadly by a mere repetition; but one sentiment was
dominant over all at the time, that I had lived a long
year in a night.

Soon after four o'clock, there suddenly stretched out
what seemed to be a reef of breakers for miles under the
sullen rain-clouds, and, with instant attention, the yawl
was put about to avoid them.

This extraordinary optical illusion was the dawn
opening on the coast, then actually ten miles away, and
in a very few minutes, as the cloud lifted, the land
seemed to rush off to its proper distance, until at last the
curtain split in two, and I found to my intense delight
that in the night we had crossed the bay!

Now came joyous sounds from our moist crew—
"Hurrah for the day! Pipe all hands to breakfast—

The voyage

slack out the mainsheet, here's the west wind"; and up
rose the sun, well washed by the torrents of rain.

An elaborate *friture* of my last three eggs was soon
cooked to perfection, and I held the frying-pan over the
side, while it drained through a fork; when, alas! there
came a heavy lurch of the boat, and all the well-

deserved breakfast was pitched into the sea, with a mild but deep-meant "Oh, how provoking!" from the hapless, hungry, lonely sailor. Shame that, preserved through such dangers, we should murmur at an omelet the less! But this tyrant stomach exacts more, and thanks less, than all the body besides.

Hastings was soon passed, and we skirted the cliffs towards Rye. I had written to the harbour-master* here to send out a boat if he saw my craft (enclosing him a sketch of it), as the entrance to that harbour seemed to be very difficult by the chart.

But the breeze was fresh and invigorating, and though sadly needing sleep after two nights without any, the idea of going to bed while such a fine breeze blew seemed preposterous, and Rye was soon left in the rear.

From this place a very low flat tongue of land stretches along in the strangest way, until at its end is the lighthouse of Dungeness. Martello towers are on the shore, but for miles outside of this, the nearest beach is all one can see; and therefore the tall lighthouse, viewed even through the glass, looked only like a small grey speck on the waves, without any land whatever between. About midday the yawl neared this very remarkable beacon, which is painted red and white; strong, lofty, and firm set on a cape of pure gravel, with here and there a house, not visible at all until you come close.

A heavy sea was here, and it was more and more as we came quite near the cape; until one fine bold wave, following our little craft, actually cast the dingey (then

---

* On December 14 this old sailor was drowned, the last of six brothers, all of whom were drowned.

towing astern) right upon the deck of the yawl, and it dealt me a severe stroke on the back, by which I was cast forward and stunned. Recovering again just in time, I saw another wave send the dingey once more on board with a crash, and splinters flew up, so we thought she was smashed, but it was the jigger-boom that was broken by the collision. The very next billow broke the dingey's painter of strong canoe rope, but much worn. Away floated the tiny cockleshell, and it was very soon hid in the trough of the sea.

"Down with the helm!"—"Haul the sheet!"—"Slack the jib!" and we gave chase in great glee, and catching her soon with the boat-hook, we quickly pulled the dingey on board, and lashed her securely down to the deck, an arrangement that answered well.

One of the great delights of real sailing is the large variety of incident that comes. Mere sitting in a yacht, while others have all the work in a breeze, and all the responsibility, is no pleasure to me; nay, I confess frankly, it is a "bore."

Once round Dungeness, we could see Folkstone and Dover cliffs; and after a few minutes of rest, to put all in readiness for a fast run before the wind, we steered straight for Dover pier.

The breeze freshened so much that the mizen had to be lowered, and as the wind was now favourable, the only thing to beware of was falling asleep; in which case the boom might jibe (swing over from one side to the other) with great force, and if it hit me on the head, then I should certainly have either a very short nap or a *very long one.**

* One of the pranks to be prepared for in a boat is this jibing of the boom, and until by practice you know the exact range of

Dover pier was, we must say, welcome to see. Often at other times we had intentionally lengthened the day's journey, in arriving near a destination sooner than it was absolutely necessary to stop the pleasure of sailing, but now we ran into Dover as fast as the flying wind would speed us.

The friends who greeted the *Rob Roy* here knew her well from a long way off, as she danced lightly over the sea; for hence had we started months ago, and here was, in one sense, the end of my voyage, as Ulysses said when alone from his raft.

> And now two nights, and now two days were past,
> Since wide I wandered on the wat'ry waste,
> Heaved on the surge with intermitting breath,
> And hourly panting in the arms of death.
>
> *Pope's* 'Odyssey,' Book V.

> Then first my eyes, by watchful toils opprest,
> Complied to take the balmy gifts of rest,
> Then first my hands did from the rudder part,
> So much the love of home possessed my heart.
>
> *Ibid.*, Book X.

I went up to the Lord Warden hotel, meaning to write home, dine, and go to bed after fifty-three hours without sleep; but while waiting for the servant to bring hot water, and with my jacket off, I tumbled on the bed for a moment—then it was 3 p.m.

Soon (as it seemed) awake again, I saw it was still

---

safety for your head in relation to that swinging spar, caution should be the rule. Long ago I had learned the exact length of the *Rob Roy's* boom in relation to my nose; for even in the Thames, soon after starting, it had once caught the back of my head, and knocked my face down on the deck, where a bloody nose (but no worse result) speedily settled the question as to which must yield when the boom and the captain are at loggerheads.

light, and with bright sun shining; also my watch had run down, the water-jug was cold, and it was a puzzle to make out how I felt so wonderfully fresh.

Why it was *next day*, and I had soundly slept for seventeen hours!

CHAPTER XVIII

Di Vernon—The Gull light—Naked Warriors—Monkey—Medway—Eyes right!—Old things—Bargees—Street boys—Young
skipper—Scene by night—Barge lingo—Holy Haven.

PERHAPS a sleep in wet clothes, such as we have
awakened from, was more likely to do harm than any
of the blasts and breezes at sea; but nothing followed,
and indeed during the whole three voyages there was
neither a head ache nor any other ache, not even a cold,
and the medicine-chest in the yawl was never opened.

Dover had been the port of departure and again of
arrival for my first canoe voyage, and the memory of
that delightful tour was recalled now by seeing a canoe
paddling in the harbour. On closer scrutiny it was per-
ceived that a young lady was its crew. Now though
there are several fair Members of our Canoe Club,
and we are quite prepared to ballot for some more, yet
the captain had not yet been fortunate enough to see
one of these canoeistes on the water, so at once the
dingey gave chase.

This was the lady's very first essay in a canoe, nevertheless, she succeeded admirably in her effort, for it is
far easier to learn a little of paddling than a little of
rowing, as every neophyte can tell you.

Henceforth I shall always know that a *Rob Roy* can
well be matched by a *Di Vernon*, and how much the
most gentle movement afloat can be refined by feminine
grace. A few hints from the older paddler in the dingey
were rapidly taken up by the apt scholar in the canoe,
while her friends rowed beside us in a boat, and at

length with that English pluck which so many English girls possess, she boldly steered into a steamer's swell, and then to the open sea, where, before a soft zephyr murmuring its undertone whispers, we hoisted her parasol for a sail, and the visitors on Dover pier had a novel treat in the duet between dingey and canoe.

Paddle and parasol

Fairly rested next day, the yawl sailed by Ramsgate Cliffs until calm and tide made us anchor in a hot baking sun.

The "Gull Lightship" was not far off, so we sculled to her in the dingey. This was the very first time I had myself actually seen the *Rob Roy* on the water with all sails set, nor dare I conceal the pride that was felt in looking at her graceful contour, her smart and sensible rig, and her snowy sails so beautifully set, as the sun-beams lit them up; viewed from a little distance, the yawl was only like a toy boat resting on a sheet of glass.

The men of the *Gull* with its red sides and red lantern masts, received me with surprise, but with most grateful thanks for books to read, and then they pressed their visitor to stop for dinner!

But he could not well feast in comfort while the *Rob Roy* was left alone and all sails up, and especially as one of the numerous vessels then drifting past (we had counted more than forty in sight at one time), seemed to be borne dangerously near to the little craft.

On this lightship there are seven men, and four more on land to relieve them regularly.* In the course of a lively conversation with their visitor, they said, "How lonely you must be!" Surely when the men exiled to a lightship pronounce the *Rob Roy* "lonely" there must be something in the charge; but my obtuse perception has not yet enabled me to find it out.

Meantime the tide had turned strongly, and my row back from the lightship in the hot sun was one of the hardest pulls I ever had, so that the lesson will not be forgotten "Stick by your ship in a tideway."

In passing along the fine gravel beach near Walmer, a curious sound was heard through the quiet haze; it was distant and continuous, but like the gabble of 10,000 ducks, and though staring hard through the binocular glass, one could only make out a confused jumble of lightish-coloured forms all in a row afar off. Soon, however, a bugle sounded the "Retire," and then it was plain that a whole regiment of soldiers were in the

* Bravely they worked to save life on the Goodwin in the fearful gale on December 1.

water bathing; their merry shouts and play had re-
sounded along the level sea, and at the bugle order they
all marched ashore in naked array, forming altogether
one of the oddest of martial sights.

The vessels now constantly crossing my course were
of all sizes, and in the quiet air we could hear their
various sounds that seemed to tell in each of a self-
contained world, where every item of life was sum-
marized on board. Men chatting, women laughing,
dogs barking, cocks crowing, and pigs squealing, a
floating farmyard, such is life on the sea. For the *Rob
Roy* I had tried to get a monkey as a funny friend, if not
as a tractable midshipman, but an end was put to the
idea by the solemn warning of an experienced comrade,
who stated, that after the first two days, a monkey
pursues steadily one line of conduct afloat—he throws
everything into the sea.

Rounding the Foreland in a lovely afternoon, we
observed how the cornfields had become ripe and
yellow, that were only growing and green when our
yawl passed the cape before. Here is the "Long Nose"
buoy again, and all the familiar landmarks, and once
more Margate, where the people warmly welcomed the
little *Rob Roy*, which they had sped on its way outward
bound with a parting cheer.

The next dawn from its grey curtain rising, saw her
sailing from Margate up the Thames, but so light was
the baffling wind, that we could not reach Sheerness
that night, and so had to anchor in five fathoms not
far from Cheney Rock, with dense fog closing round,
and the Nore gong ringing, while my bright little cabin
glowed with comfort, and the newspapers were studied
in peace. Thence sailing into Sheerness and up to

Queenborough, we anchored close by the Coastguard hulk, in safe and quiet waters. Sunday was a delicious rest, and the dingey took me aboard the hulk, where a number of sailors and their large families living, give a very remarkable appearance to the vessel 'tween decks. The children were delighted to receive books and pictures, and until late in the dark the infantile menagerie squalled with all their might.

An expedition of river discovery up the Medway seemed to be worth trying now, for no bonds of time or engagements fettered that glorious freedom of action which is one of the prize features of sailing thus. The yawl went bowling along on this new errand amid huge old hulks, tall-masted frigates, black warrior-like ironclads, gay yachts, odoriferous fishing-smacks, and a fleet of steady, brown-sailed, business-like barges. This is a pleasant and a cheerful river for some days' excursion, with a mild excitement in sailing over banks and shoals, and yet not striking once, although we had no chart.

The tide helps much, until the high ground near Chatham adds rock and sylvan scenes to the flat banks of the winding estuary.

Now we come on a busy industry of peculiar type, thousands of convicts working on the new sea-wall, closely guarded by armed keepers. These poor criminals are paid or privileged according to their good behaviour, and it has been found that their labour thus stimulated is very productive.

Once fairly up among the warships at Chatham, the *Rob Roy* anchors by the Powder Magazine, and while a waterman rows away for the usual supplies—"Two eggs, pat of butter, and *The Times*"—we inspect the

Royal Engineers as they are engaged alongside at
pontooning, and are frequently pulled up by the command of a smart sergeant—"Eyes—right," for they *will*
take furtive glances at my dingey gyrating so, as they
had never seen boat spin round before. The comment
on the dingey's shape was ventured, too, "It's for hall
the world like 'alf a hegg."

Pushing on again, still up the river, the *Rob Roy* had to
beat against an east wind all through the densely
packed brigs and barges in the narrow bend at
Rochester, where the difficulty of working her added
zest to the journey, and now and then a resounding
crash from some great barge drifting down against
other vessels, told me that not every one of the craft was
as fortunate in navigation as the yawl. Before us is the
Cathedral, but it is far too stiff in its sharp outline to
arrest the eye for a moment. On the other side, the fine
old weather-worn and time-eaten Castle rears its great
tower, and challenges a long and satisfying look,
especially as this was the only ancient ruin we had seen
in the tour, and so there had long been a yearning in the
mind for such, just as there is when you travel in Norway or America, until at last the hunger for old things
becomes ravenous and intolerable.

The yawl's mast will be able to pass under the bridge,
for the tide is low, and beyond it now we are in sunny
green fields, and sailing on smoothly amid quiet villages,
rich pastures, and the exuberant hop-grounds of
thoroughly English Kent.

Three boys bathing from a boat came near, and for a
treat we took them on board, while their hair dripped
wet and their teeth chattered fast after too long a swim,
but they had read the name on my white flag, and they

had also read two canoe books, and so for miles they devoured all that was said and shown on the yawl, then thanking much because they were "awfully glad," and they rowed home. How pleasant it is to give pleasure to boys!

The *Rob Roy* got aground only once in this trip above the bridge, and that only for five minutes, which except the bump on a rock at Bembridge, was her sole mishap of this sort, an immunity quite extraordinary from the seaman's dreaded foe, the shore. The barges that were now floating up the crowded Medway interested me exceedingly, and acquaintance was readily made with their inhabitants almost every day for the next three weeks, until it became evident that "Barge Life" is a stratum of society quite as full of character and incident as any other, and wide open for examination by those who would study a *genus* of mankind very little known. Large and important duties are entrusted to these men; rich cargoes are committed to their honesty and skill; families live on barges by thousands, and the coasting journey of a barge is by no means an easy thing or a dull one. We must not judge of them by those great black boxes full of coals, that float on the water above London Bridge, with one man and a long oar, and yet even a coal barge is worth watching.

In the dank mist of a dull November evening it will drift unseen past the Temple Gardens. Wonderful sounds launch into the fog from an invisible shouter on board, whose "Tom" or "Bill" on a wharf ashore instantly knows the call, and answers. Then there is a colloquy loud and public in the extreme, yet utterly private in its meaning to anyone besides the two who are talking. It is only paralleled by the shrill interjections of

London street boys calling to each other across the Strand, of which the grown-up public cannot make out one syllable, but which the stratum below them of three feet high is perfectly contented with, discerning every word.

The barges that trade to the Medway are fine, strong sea-boats; their sailing qualities are excellent, and they are improved every year by a regatta specially for them, where forty gay-dressed, bluff, and burly craft compete for prizes. In this match the utmost of skill, sharpened by years of river sailing, is shown in wind and tide, and knowledge of intricate channels, and among such competitors "fouling is fair."

As the yawl glides on the water among hayricks and whetting scythes, one of these gallant barges floats beside us with the name on its stern—S.E.C.P.T.E.R.— dubious in import, we allow, whether it means that the stout matter-of-fact lighter has been christened as a shadowy ghost, or a royal symbol. The veriest urchin steers her, with a little fat hand on the heavy tiller twelve feet long, and a hunk of good rye-bread in his other fist. Now and then he sings out in a thin soprano, "Fayther, boat's a'ead," and his father (hidden below), answers deep-toned, from the cabin, "Keep 'er away, lad." From him I asked, "How old is your boy?" and the parent's head popped up to see, but it was the child that smartly answered, "Eight years old." He looked five. Round the next reach the barge bears down, and shakes her sails in the wind to arrest progress a little. They have come near home, but not to stop. It is only their country house, and up steps the bargee mother from out her small *boudoir* in the cabin below, and jumping heavily into a boat, she pulls ashore

to where a little girl is meekly waiting ready for orders—
"Get the fish directly, Hagnes," and the daughter runs
off fleetly and back soon, and the mother is speedily
aboard again—all this marketing being done while the
barge has been drifting slowly past, and then her sails
are filled to continue the voyage.

Night fell, and the yawl anchored by a soft green
field, with the bowsprit among the rushes. Bright
furnaces for lime and plaster-works show here and
there around, and they roared and blazed up fitfully
with waving jets of flame, like the ironworks in Shrop-
shire, while the reflections glittered on the river, and
reddened long reaches in a glow. The barges kept
streaming by in the dark laden with rich commerce,
and merry, singing crews—a very curious scene. To
them the *Rob Roy*, of course, looked quite as strange, and
one hailed us gruffly—"Who're you?" answer, "I'm the
Rob Roy!"—"What in the world did you come here for?"
"To look at the beautiful lights on your river." In a
murmuring grumble, he said to that, "Too many on
'em there is—we can't see where we're goin' with
them"; and this is indeed perfectly true, for the light of
these furnaces dazzles by its brightness, which is not
diffused, whereas if no lights were there at all, the men
could see well enough, for it is marvellous how the eye
will perceive at least the bounds between land and
water, when practice sharpens keen vision and no false
light is shining. It is, however, quite true also, that the
language of the barge-world is not to be found complete
in Johnson's *Dictionary*. It is far more powerful than
elegant. Words that are unused ashore except in anger
or the coarsest abuse seem to be the gentle appellations
of endearment between father and sons afloat. But we

must not forget that it is the meaning attached to a word by speaker and hearer, and not that given to it by a world outside of both, which the word will represent.*

From the highest point we could reach towards Maidstone, we soon ran down again to Rochester, and various were the conflicting verdicts of bargees as to whether or not my mast would now go under the bridge, for the tide was very high, and I sailed back and forward, getting opinions, and surveying the bridge on all sides. At length I determined it could be done, and my heart beat nervously as the yawl neared the centre arch—not as to danger, but the dishonour of breaking a goodly spar at the end of a cruise, and in so trumpery a feat. It passed clear, however, by inches.

The evening was too fine at Sheerness to think of anchoring yet, and with sudden resolve we set off again to Southend. Here the advice of a yacht lying near was followed foolishly (get *facts* from experts and decide on deeds yourself), for I anchored without sounding, and too late found it was in shallow water, only eight feet by the lead, and the tide running out. To bed but not to sleep, for the water sunk to five feet, and, angry with myself, I roused at one o'clock, gave out all the rope, sheered off shore by the rudder, and then, again at rest, gained only six inches of depth; but once more sounding, there was only six inches to spare under the keel and with a strong breeze on shore. Therefore, once more on

---

* The use of the word "bloody" is now general among the lowest classes all over England. The meaning intended by this is not what scholars would agree to. Hundreds of times the word is employed only for "very," and it is strange how soon one's first shudders at the sound become faint, and even die.

the move, we fastened the inner end of the cable to the larger anchor and heaved this out, and then payed out all the chain, and sheered with the rudder, but still she was in shoal water. Finally, as the wind increased, I had to haul in both anchors and shove out into the deep, and thus, by omitting to do right at once what was easy at the time, the whole night had been consumed by intervals of wet and needless trouble.

Life in the yawl had now become such a pleasant life, that to leave it was a duty deferred as long as possible. We ranged several times up and down the Thames, visiting many an old nook, well known in former days; Holy Haven, for instance; it was eighteen years since we had harboured there in a little sailing-boat and spent a night with a collier captain, and learned more of coals and colliers than one could read in a week. This was done by keeping him resolutely on the point the man knew all about until he was quite pumped dry. This nice little refuge-harbour is the one I like best in all the river. Only one house—no bother from shore folks, deep channel, and clean sand to anchor in. If it were not for this narrow and safe retreat, there would often be hard times in stormy days between Gravesend and Sheerness.

．　．　．　．　．　．　．

By the desire of the *Chichester* Committee I joined the *Dolphin*[1] at Sheerness, and with a regular salt captain,

[1] [A letter written to *The Times* by MacGregor had resulted in the gift of the *Dolphin*, a 20-ton sailing cutter, for use by the boys of the training ship *Chichester*.]

and a seaman from the Bendigo diggings, and a boy from the *Chichester*, we weighed the cutter's anchor to bring the prize to Greenhithe.

The pier-man smiled gladly on the gift yacht. The taut Guard-ship bristling with big guns seemed to look down kindly on the little vessel, and even the grim old hulks, otherwise sulky enough, appeared to wish her well as she loosed her white sails to a gentle breeze. Yes, and the sun smiled brightly, too, with a balmy day like summer again.

Barges flocked out, clustering on the water as in my former visits here, but the *Dolphin* mingled with them not as in a mere play, but with a benign and holy purpose in her gait, for it was the gracious breath of Christian benevolence that wafted the *Dolphin* on. She was a present to the homeless boys, and so a gift that shall be one time repaid by the Friend of the friendless with measure "running over."

Yantlet was passed and the Blythe and Jenkin, when sunset shrouded sleeping Father Thames. Then the ship-lights sparkled numerous on the stream and red rays from the beacons glinted athwart our sail. Swift steamers whisked by in the dark. Tall, gaunt, sailing-ships rustled their dusky canvas, and struggling little tug-boats rattled with instant paddle as they passed.

Clouds withdrew from above as we neared the *Chichester*, and the full moon came out and looked upon the "gift for boys" with her long pendant streaming in the mild and onward breeze.

Then, to me silent, lying on the deck as if in a summer eve, came many-coloured thoughts—the *Rob Roy*'s rovings by river and sea in brightsome days and thundering nights, the good seed sown by the shore, the thousand incidents of a charming voyage.

But best of them all was the sail in the *Dolphin*.

We may begin in faith, and continue in hope, but greatest of the three is charity in

THE END

APPENDIX

A letter from John MacGregor giving his first account of the crossing from Havre.

Littlehampton July 25 [1867]

I AM in extreme enjoyment. In a charming hotel of the old quiet comfortable type with a nice landlady— After a delicious sleep on a soft bed the first good rest I have had for exactly 14 days because of the horrid bustle on the river & in the ports from 1 a.m. each morning—an English egg breakfast & then to find my yacht is aground as I woke too late to move her before the tide fell so perforce I must remain a whole day & night more here & why not—why rush away. I need no more hurry. A load is off my mind—I had set [myself] a great feat to do, a greater one now seen in the past than in prospect & I have been allowed full gratification of success.

Pride and satisfaction too much for such a worldly matter may supervene but I must only guard against excess—there is a legitimate amount allowable.

In a brief note yesterday I wrote that I have sailed across from Havre 100 miles—& much more by the winding route I had taken & now I will give more details & to save me entering them again in my journal please keep this letter that I may have it again.

Well I was puzzled how to get back.—to go by the French coast again would be tedious and dangerous.— The S.W. wind favourable for this route back is put down in the Pilot book as "very dangerous for vessels off Cape d'Antifer" and if I waited for an E or N.E. wind I sh'd have to beat all the way.

Thoroughly assured of the splendid sea qualities of the R [the *Rob Roy*] I preferred to risk my sleep and comfort of one or two long nights at sea to the safety of my boat entering harbour again every night for a week & on the 23d I made up my mind to start next mg if there was any kind of wind.

Having gone to bed I could not sleep.—And having put away my Pilot book Vol 3 of the English coast (as usual) so safely that I could not find it I had to buy a French one & French chart—Their book was so stupidly put together that 3 hours of hot work with it pulled it to pieces and lucky am I that I did not much need it.

Happily I have found this mg my English one so I am all right now.

About 2 a.m. on the 24th I looked out of my cabin on a calm harbour with a gleaming moon but scud drifting across with an E wind—Vessels began to move. A big English 3 master had its crew weighing anchor with a fine sea song & I had now to make up my mind & it was "Yes I will go"—and why wait for Sunlight? Why not get all ready by the moon. So without a wink of sleep I got up cooked a coffee breakfast & the leg of a chicken pumped everything perfectly dry examined every rope & spar & found my bowsprit had been smashed at the end by my collision with the 2 steamers 2 nights before but still it *seemed* strong enough.

At 3 I quietly cast off my line from the fishing smack I had been fast to & rowed down into the harbour mouth. Here there was a fresh breeze but lo it had now changed to S.W. (the wind that raises a sea) but quite favourable if you don't mind a good tossing.

The only danger in a stern wind is that if by any mishap I should fall overboard the yacht would leave me—In a head wind it would soon "come up to the wind" & I might by swimming catch it again but with a S.W. wind (& course N.) this w'd be hopeless.—It may be said why not tie yourself to the boat? Well if the rope is short you are too confined—if it is long say 6 feet & you fall out you may be dragged under water by it or hopelessly entangled. A good suggestion has been made by a boy here to have it a long rope wound on a stiff reel so it would check gradually and give time. This is very good and if *again* I try a long voyage I will adopt this plan.

In getting out of harbour I moved slowly against the wind & at last called out to two men to bring a boat.— They came—Will you tow me to the pier end?—Yes Give us 10 francs first—No its too much—Well, eight— Yes I'll give that. So they hooked on. Presently "You had better give us the 'argent' now—the sea will be too rough soon to come alongside you. 'Yes' said I but lo I had only 4 francs in change besides Napoleons—"Give us a 20 franc piece & we will send you the change"— "No but I will give you an order on M. Mancin's the yacht agent at Havre for 5 francs"—They agreed & I loosened the hatch got out paper wrote the order & put it in an envelope & gave it & the money to the men!

It was anxious work towing out at night while a dozen huge luggers were going too & all bobbing about—at length they called out "Get ready your mizzen sail—hoist" & up it went. "Get ready your jib"

& then at a critical moment "Hoist" & up it went but in an instant the bowsprit broke and the jib went flapping up like a balloon or an umbrella inside out.

That was indeed a supreme disaster & for a moment I thought "Well it shows I must turn back" But when

they called out "Voulez vous sortir encore?" I said firmly "Oui!"—Hauled down the jib, put two reefs in it, & fastened it to the stem end & dashed splendidly past the lighthouse with a bound & a plunge. I made up my mind to go on for 2 or 3 hours & if I found it w'd not do I could come back to harbour—But it did well enough & happened to be the best sail I could have carried with a leading wind now fine & fresh so I said at last Here goes for old England & lighted up my compass & stood N by ½ East.

In an hour I was free of Cape de la Heve & in the dawn of day saw I had the wind exactly right for the Isle of Wight so I cracked on gloriously. The same for hours. The R [*Rob Roy*] 'took her seas' in splendid style—only a few came over in the first ½ hour & wet me completely through for I had not put on my oilskin trousers & coat as I meant to have rowed in the lighter dress & then to moor & put on the bad weather suit.

However the wetting dried by 10 a.m. in the sun & at

12 all sight of land was lost & I did not see any land again till 4 a.m. next day. Very few ships to be seen & all of them far far away—Only one solitary gull in the whole voyage. It was a little lonely but my eye on the compass kept me with a companion & I cooked another breakfast now & till 6 p.m. I began to feel horribly sleepy. Several times I fell into a nap & was only rudely wakened by the boat coming to the wind & a wave slapping me rudely in the face or the jib giving an angry rattle. But to provide against accidents (for I am abundantly cautious) when I felt the sleepy fits coming on I wound a rope round my arm & across my body so as not at any rate to be jerked out of the boat asleep. Some mushrooms I had eaten the day before disagreed with me sadly & we parted company; when it was time to take a nip of brandy and another meal.

The wind held good until I had made about 60 miles & then it fell off. Now I did indeed feel lonely. Tossed about in a fine rolling swell but without wind & with the disagreeable feeling it might now turn right in my teeth when it would be utterly impossible to reach England under 48 hours. In an hour or so the wind began

again all right as before. I had stood up every 5 minutes on deck holding fast by the mizen shrouds to see the breeze coming—I had also meantime taken my axe (a sharp one always within reach of my right hand) run forward, chopped the lashings of the bowsprit, hauled it in, rigged up the stump, shaken out the 2 reefs from the sail & secured it to the stump so I was able again to set full sail & felt thoroughly proud of doing it all so well.

From then to night the wind gradually increased & was just right for me though here they called it a gale— The Rob Roy is made for a strong breeze. I scanned the horizon with my glass to see land—none! none! then when sunset came I scanned again for any single lighthouse, none!—it was too thick to leeward to see them or it shewed I was at least 20 miles off.—Now it began to be cold. But I went on & [on] until heavy banks of clouds threatened [?] round—a big three-master loomed up & I went close & hailed "How far to the Nab light" but no answer came. At last after much reasoning I came to the conclusion I must pass the night at sea—I could not risk coming near to the Needles or the cliffs of the I of Wight when the lights were invisible & thus if I had to lie to & try & sleep it was safest to do so far from land so as not to drift on shore in the dark.

I lowered the mainsail & "hove to" under jib & mizen & she rode beautifully to it. Still to make it even better & to ensure my not drifting northwards I struck the jib & threw out an anchor which kept her head to wind & there was the most delightful easy rise & fall at each sea without one splash on board.

I had lighted my sea lamp & now I coiled up in the well (3 feet by 3 feet) & tried to sleep. But it was too cramped—Then I tried to get out my dingey from the cabin so as to lie down there but on second thoughts felt if the wind increased it would only waken me when the sea was too high to get the dingey in again or if a collision *did* occur it would be bad to be below. Finally I adopted a plan which answered admirably & by means of which I think I could pass a week in my boat in safety & (reasonable) comfort—I closed everything up, put on (or kept on) my life jacket & oilskin put the lamp close down to the deck near my face (it seemed a pleasant companion) wrapped myself in the mainsail & so arranged it that while I could lie at full length I yet could not fall overboard. In an instant I was sound asleep & never in my life did I sleep better! Fancy this in a wet night on a boat's deck lying to in a heavy sea, but the seas were long & rolling & not angry or short. Some of the rollers were 3 in a mile. Oddly enough I had very agreeable dreams several of which I tried to remember but they passed away. One or two vessels passed me near enough to see their lights but though they looked like companions for a few minutes I felt it shewed I was in the track of ships and therefore more dangerous for being run down. However my light was an excellent one made after my own plan with a good big Palmer candle far nicer than oil.

I awoke suddenly & behold the sun in the heavens—Where am I? & I turned my head and oh delightful sight there was the English coast.—Three cheers burst from the crew, three more, & three more still. Hurrah for old England my voyage is accomplished!

I sung away cheerily while I boiled 2 eggs & crammed in all the tea the teapot would hold—hoisted the British flag on one mast & the Rob Roy flag on the other & thanked God most fervently for the mercy of a good night's rest (four hours of sleep) & health & spirits perfectly restored.

APPENDIX

I had forgotten to wind up my watch but it must have been about 6.30 by the sun & now I set all sail & coming near land found it perfectly impossible to know in the very least whether I was to the East or the West of the Isle of Wight.

Presently 4 noble 3 deckers came steaming up & several iron-clads but I could not reach them to find out my place & so at 11 a.m. came to the nearest port but it was not like any one of the pictures in the stupid French Pilot book. However I approached carefully— bumped the ground in trying to get in, so shoved out & anchored. A fishing boat came near. "Ahoy what's the name of this place?" "Littlehampton Sir." So I found I had drifted about 20 miles during the night & to the west [actually to the east] just as I wished & I soon tore in, anchored, & lay down in the hot sun under my boat's awning for one of the most charming sleeps a weary man could have.

This little place is a quiet sandy beach with children & spades & among the first visitors two came who turned out to be choristers of the Temple church whose faces I see every Sunday! They had read the canoe book & so they came to see the Rob Roy. They gave me an English paper & I put my boat in order & had a read. Then at the hotel the young waiter "Charlie" was dying to get a canoe. One of our Club had put up there for 3 days having come round the English coast all this way in his canoe! I was glad to be able to give a copy of the book to this lad when I sat down to roast duck & peas and British beer & turned in to a soft bed with sheets a luxury I had not used since at Dieppe exactly one month ago!

Quiet repose & a walk on the sands & a resolve to

stop another night here then tomorrow I hope to sail on to the Isle of Wight & stop there at Mr. White's & get a good many alterations made in the boat & sail about there & in Southampton Water &c &c & take my time homewards for the Thames.—All this future part is perfectly easy work.—The harbours are all good for entry—the West wind (the prevailing one) exactly favourable till I round the Foreland again—& no hurry required as was the case in going out to France where the hardest part was always awaiting me about rounding Cape d'Antifer before the wind changed.

I feel I have performed a feat & no more need be added to it—It is worthy of the Captain of the Canoe Club & I am content.

[Here the letter ends, the paper being torn across, leaving only a small segment of a circle on the edge of which MacGregor had begun to scribble the points of the compass. The letter is written on four sheets of paper, two with the crest of the Canoe Club and one with that of the Athenæum.]